Jacket Jazz

E N C O R E

That Patchwork Place®

Six More Great Looks...Over 30 Patchwork Techniques

by Judy Murrah

CREDITS

Editor-in-Chief . . . . Barbara Weiland
Managing Editor . . . . Greg Sharp
Copy Editor . . . . Liz McGehee
Proofreaders . . . . Tina Cook
Leslie Phillips
Design Director . . . . Judy Petry
Text and Cover Designer . . . . Joanne Lauterjung
Photographer . . . . Brent Kane
Photo Stylist . . . . Susan Jones
Illustrators . . . . Laurel Strand
Stephanie Benson

Jacket Jazz ©
© 1994 by Judy Murrah
That Patchwork Place, Inc., PO Box 118, Bothell, WA 98041-0118 USA

Printed in Hong Kong
99 98 97 96 95 94   6 5 4 3 2 1

The information in this book is presented in good faith, but no warranty is given nor results guaranteed. Since That Patchwork Place, Inc., has no control over choice of materials or procedures, the company assumes no responsibility for the use of this information.

MISSION STATEMENT

WE ARE DEDICATED TO PROVIDING QUALITY PRODUCTS THAT ENCOURAGE CREATIVITY AND PROMOTE SELF-ESTEEM IN OUR CUSTOMERS AND OUR EMPLOYEES.

WE STRIVE TO MAKE A DIFFERENCE IN THE LIVES WE TOUCH.

That Patchwork Place is an employee-owned, financially secure company.

Library of Congress Cataloging-in-Publication Data

Murrah, Judy
    Jacket jazz encore : six more great looks—over 30 patchwork techniques / by Judy Murrah.
       p. cm.
    ISBN 1-56477-069-9 :
    1. Coats. 2. Patchwork—Patterns. 3. Quilted goods. I. Title.
TT535.M88   1994
746.46'0432—dc20
                                                        94-29985
                                                        CIP

Dedication

To my dear, kind, and special friends and staff members at Quilts, Inc., who have become a lovable, caring, and supportive family.

Acknowledgments

My deep appreciation goes to:

My editor, Barbara Weiland, and her staff;

That Patchwork Place President, Nancy J. Martin;

Cheryl Greider Bradkin, Nancy Brenan Daniel, Marilyn Doheny, Linda Fiedler, Betty Gall, and Kaye Wood for their techniques and inspiration over the years;

The Texas shops: Great Expectations, Quilts, Inc. (713) 496-1366 in Houston; Rebbecca's Fabric Shoppe (512) 782-2173 in Edna; and Sew What Bernina (409) 892-7574 in Beaumont, where they give each of my students special attention in selecting their jacket fabrics. Also to Sew Much More (512) 452-3166 in Austin and Sewing Machines by B & B (512) 573-4668 in Victoria, where my students have received invaluable sewing machine assistance. Each of these stores also carries the special tools in the shopping lists for each jacket. If any of the supplies listed in this book are not available in your area, call one of these stores. They will be happy to assist you.

Also, Bernina of America, Inc.; Elna, Inc; Quilter's Rule International, Inc.; Omnigrid, Inc.; Fasco/Fabric Sales Co. Inc.; Hoffman California Fabrics; John Kaldor Fabricmaker U.S.A., Ltd.; Quilter's Resource, Inc.; Fabri-Quilt, Inc.; Fons-Porter Designs; and Mission Valley/Westpoint.

Table of Contents

Introduction

My first book, *Jacket Jazz,* has succeeded beyond my wildest imaginings. The folks at That Patchwork Place must have guessed how successful it would be because they were talking about book number two before number one was off the press. It is a joy to know that so many of you purchased the first book and have become "Jacket Jazz Groupies!" I have enjoyed seeing you in your jackets at quilt shows and exhibits, and it has been fun to receive your letters and phone calls. I have even been able to get to know some of you through my Mystery Jacket Correspondence Course.

Jacket Jazz Encore includes five different jacket looks plus a vest. It was written using a format similar to that in *Jacket Jazz,* so those of you who have used the first book can jump right in. Designing these five jackets was not difficult for me because I have many more ideas on paper and in my head than I could ever use. I'm just thrilled you want more!

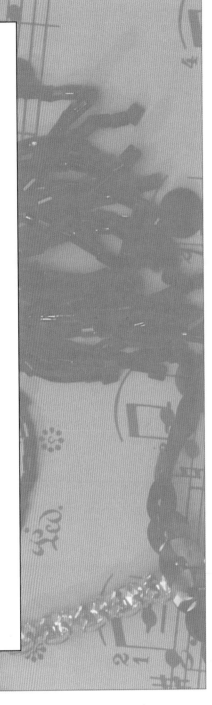

The task of designing the jackets, teaching classes on them to work out the kinks, and writing this book was demanding, to say the least. My students have been helpful in pointing out what they liked about my instructions and also where they needed a little more clarification. Because of their loyalty, I did manage to teach several classes on each jacket before the manuscript was due.

So here you go again. You have five brand new jackets plus a vest to make. I hope you enjoy them as much as you did the first five. Let me hear from you. If you would like to receive information on my Mystery Jacket, write to me at: 109 Pasadena Dr., Victoria, TX 77904, and include a SASE.

Judy Murrah

Each of the jacket styles is based on the same basic shape with variations in the neckline treatment, jacket length, and the shaping at the bottom edge. The sleeves are easy enough for a beginner to attach to an open armhole, in the same way that a sleeve is sewn to the armhole of a shirt.

Choose your favorite jacket from the styles shown below. If you are a beginner, I recommend you start with Jacket Eight since the patchwork pieces are a little less complex than those in the other jackets. (By the way, the jacket number has nothing to do with the degree of difficulty: it's just the order in which I designed and taught them. Jackets One through Five appear in my first book, *Jacket Jazz*.)

NOTE: As my students experiment with my jackets and the patchwork techniques, many of them play "mix and match," choosing their favorite jacket style and then applying the patchwork pieces of their choice. Some of the jackets shown in the photos in this book are a result of this play, so they are not exactly like the pattern. If this approach appeals to you, you have my encouragement to play to your heart's content. However, I suggest that you follow one of my "recipes" for your first jacket. As you gain skill and confidence, you can create your own variations, perhaps using an already-favorite jacket pattern for the foundation in place of the ones on the pull-out pattern insert at the back of this book.

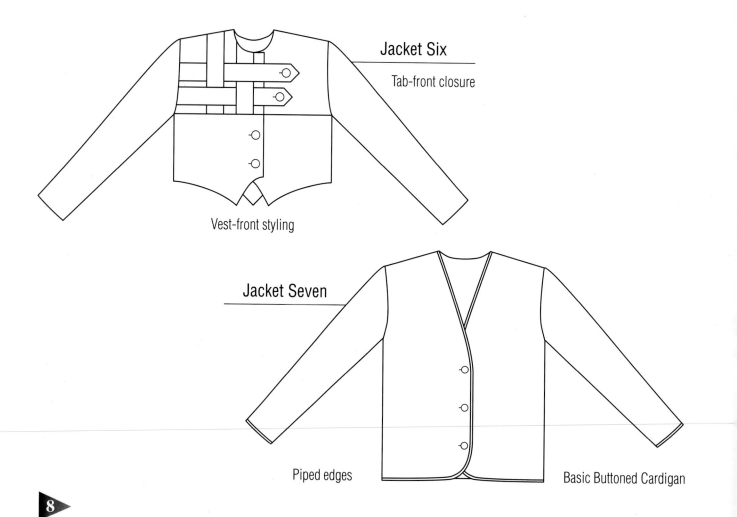

Jacket Six

Tab-front closure

Vest-front styling

Jacket Seven

Piped edges

Basic Buttoned Cardigan

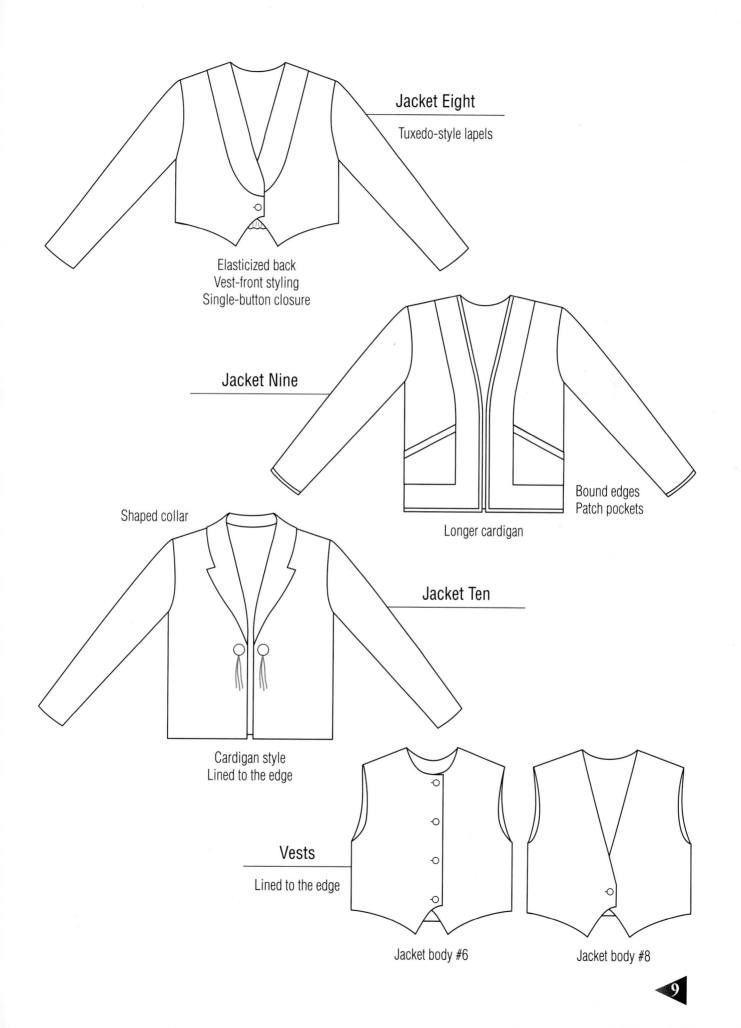

Jacket Eight

Tuxedo-style lapels

Elasticized back
Vest-front styling
Single-button closure

Jacket Nine

Bound edges
Patch pockets

Longer cardigan

Shaped collar

Jacket Ten

Cardigan style
Lined to the edge

Vests

Lined to the edge

Jacket body #6

Jacket body #8

✓ *Pattern Piece Overview*

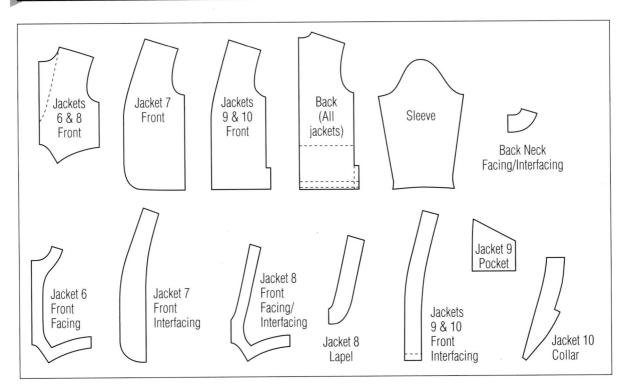

To make it possible to give patterns for the five different jackets and one vest, I started with a basic shape, then lengthened or shortened it, cut a point at the bottom edge or left it straight, and changed the neckline treatment.

The jacket pattern pieces are printed on the pullout pattern insert at the back of the book and are multi-sized, with cutting lines marked for five sizes: Petite (6-8); Small (10-12); Medium (14-16); Large (18-20); and Extra Large (22-24). See Jacket Sizing on page 11.

You will find a jacket front pattern piece for Jackets Six and Eight, another front for Jacket Seven, and finally one for Jackets Nine and Ten. There is one pattern piece for the jacket back, with cutting lines indicated for each jacket, plus three back neck facing pattern pieces and one sleeve pattern piece.

Lapel pattern pieces for Jacket Eight and the collar for Jacket Ten are also included on the pullout pattern insert, along with the front facings and interfacing pieces required for each jacket and the pocket for Jacket Nine.

If you would like, you may use the body of Jacket Six or Eight for a vest instead of using a commercial vest pattern. If you wish to wear your vest over blouses and T-shirts with deep armholes, stitch a deeper seam in the armhole from notch to notch under the arm.

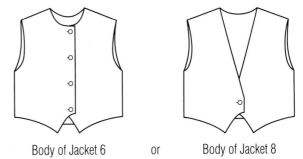

Body of Jacket 6   or   Body of Jacket 8

To preserve the original pattern pieces for later use, trace each pattern piece for the jacket you are making onto tracing paper, following the lines for your size.

♪ **NOTE:** All seam allowances are ½" wide unless otherwise noted.

Since cutting lines for five different lengths on each jacket (one for each size) would be confusing, a lengthen/shorten line is printed on the jacket front and back pattern pieces so that you can customize the pattern to a length that is comfortable on your figure. If you are petite, you will probably want to shorten the jacket front and back pattern pieces in two locations before cutting; if you are extra tall, you may want to lengthen them using the lower set of lines on the pattern pieces. Check the sleeve length, too, and lengthen or shorten as needed.

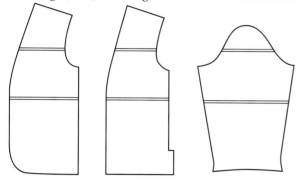

Adjust pattern pieces for correct length using the lengthen/shorten lines.

When tracing the sleeve in your size, be sure to mark the shoulder notch and the dots on the sleeve and the armhole notches on the jacket front, back, and sleeve for matching purposes when sewing.

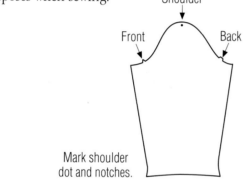

Mark shoulder dot and notches.

✓ Jacket Sizing

These jackets are a littler closer fitting than those in *Jacket Jazz*. They have a slightly extended shoulder and a slightly lowered armhole for comfort. To choose your size, check the sizing chart on this page, using your bust measurement as the guide. It is also a good idea to measure the pattern at the full hip and calculate the *finished* hip measurement. Compare it to your own to make sure the jacket will be large enough. It should be at least 3" to 4" larger than your hips for wearing ease. If not, adjust the pattern to fit your figure before cutting pieces from the foundation fabric.

Sizing Chart		
	BUST	HIP
Petite (6–8)	29"–32"	32"–34½"
Small (10–12)	33"–35"	35½"–37"
Medium (14–16)	36"–38½"	38½"–40½"
Large (18–20)	39½"–42½"	41½"–44½"
Extra Large (22–24)	43"–46"	45"–48"

After tracing the pattern pieces (front, back, and sleeve) for the jacket you are making in the selected size, cut them from the tissue and pin together along the ½" seam lines. Try on to check the fit.

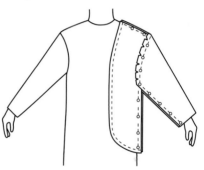

If you feel the pattern is too large, unpin the tissue, reposition the pieces over the master pattern and trace the next smaller size.

You can also adjust the fit once the patchwork pieces have been made and attached to the jacket foundation. Simply taper the side seams from the underarm down to the bottom edge of the jacket if it seems too large. You may taper the sleeves, too, if you like a closer fit at the wrist. For a shapelier fit in Jackets 6 and 8, as well as in the vest, you can also nip in the waist.

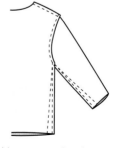

Taper side seams and underarm seams for a closer fit at hips and wrist.

✓Recipe for a Successful Jacket

Making one of my jackets is a little like following a recipe. First you cut the pieces for the foundation jacket, then you make and attach the patchwork pieces. Next, you embellish your work as desired, covering all raw edges with pretty trims. Finally, you add a lining that is easy to attach and covers the wrong side of the foundation for a finished look and for wearing comfort. Follow the recipe, and the results will be a wonderful, wearable work of art.

1. Study the photos shown for each jacket and select your favorite.

2. Before you go shopping, read through "General Materials" on pages 13–14. These are things you will need to make each of the jackets.

3. After you decide which jacket to make, refer to the "Shopping List" for that particular jacket. Assemble all your supplies and materials before you begin.

4. Before you start one of the jackets, read through "Jacket Construction—General Directions" on pages 15–17. Although each jacket style requires some variation in construction, each one starts out and is put together in basically the same way.

5. Next, examine the photo of the jacket you want to make in the section called "Construction at a Glance."

6. Be sure to save the false starts, rejects, and scraps from your patchwork pieces, then turn to page 106 and use them to make a very special vest. In this section, you will also learn five more quick-piecing techniques to use the scraps for more patchwork.

✓General Materials

No matter which of the five jackets you decide to make, you will need the following materials and tools.

JACKET FABRICS

Jacket Foundation Fabric—2¹/₂ yards of cotton flannel or muslin. It is easier to work with flannel because your patchwork pieces will cling to it better than to muslin. However, flannel is warmer than muslin, so if you live in a warm climate, you may want to use muslin instead.

Jacket Lining—2¹/₂ yards smooth, lightweight fabric. A silky lining fabric gives a more professional look and makes the jacket easier to slip on and off, but smooth cotton prints are more exciting peeking out when you remove your jacket. For the best of both worlds, use a cotton fabric in the jacket body and a silky lining in the sleeves!

Interfacing—³/₈ to ¹/₂ yard of a lightweight fusible interfacing. This adds support and prevents stretching around the neckline and the bottom edge of the jacket. Collars also require interfacing. You will need a press cloth as well, and a copy of the manufacturer's fusing directions.

Large Pieces of Pattern Tracing Paper or Pattern Tracing Cloth—Full-size pattern pieces are on the pullout pattern insert at the back of this book. Trace the pattern pieces in the proper size for the jacket you are making.

Upholstery gimp, braid, bias tape, or other flat, decorative trim—You will need several yards of ¹/₂"- to ⁵/₈"-wide trim to cover the edges of the patchwork pieces after they are attached to the jacket foundation. Check the shopping list for the jacket you are making.

Shoulder pads—I like raglan-style shoulder pads to support the weight of the jacket and to minimize my hip line! I insert them between the patchwork jacket and the lining, so they do not need to be covered. There is room in this jacket for shoulder pads that are ³/₈" to ³/₄" thick, depending on the shape of your shoulders.

Thread—Make sure you have thread in colors to match braid, lining, and fashion fabrics.

Fusible web—You will need this for some of the patchwork pieces. (Check the "Shopping List" for the jacket you are making.) Choose either Wonder-Under, a web attached to a release paper, or Fine Fuse, a web without release paper that requires the use of a Teflon press cloth.

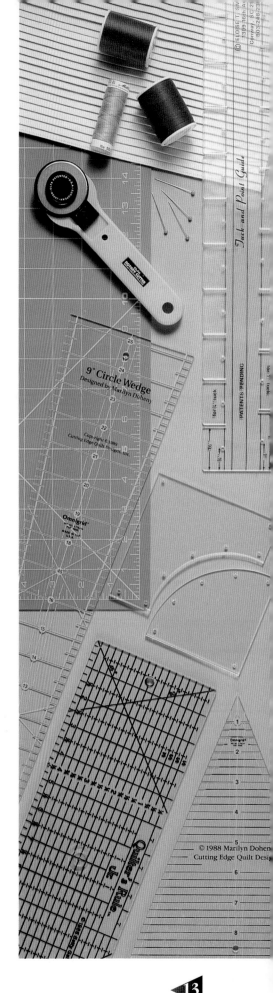

TOOLS

Zigzag sewing machine with the following optional attachments. The numbers in parentheses are the Bernina feet numbers, but these feet are available for most other machines as well.

Braiding Foot (#21), Tricot Foot (#12), ¼" Patchwork Foot (#37), Piping Foot (#38).

Rotary cutter, mat, and rulers

FABRIC SELECTION FOR THE PATCHWORK PIECES

Making one of these jackets is the perfect excuse to go fabric shopping. It gives you a chance to use lots of fabrics in the colors you love. Start by choosing the jacket you want to make and study the photos for fabric ideas. Specific suggestions for fabric selection for each jacket are included with the shopping lists. Take this book with you to the store for reference.

For easiest handling, select 100% cotton fabrics. When using other fabrics such as lamé, you will need to back them with a lightweight woven fusible interfacing before you do any cutting or sewing. I do not recommend prewashing any of the fabrics as they will lose body and will be more difficult to handle. If your fabrics have been prewashed, treat them with a little spray-on starch to add body while you work with them.

Following are the general guidelines for fabric selection that I share with my students in class. If you have a local fabric store with knowledgeable staff, ask for their assistance, too.

1. Decide how you will wear your jacket and the mood you wish to create. Will you wear it with denim skirts and jeans for casual, everyday attire, or with a skirt or dress for work? Would you rather make it for special occasions, such as holiday events? Choose fabrics that will create the desired effect.

   For casual wear or work, denims, solids, and calm prints are appropriate. For an evening out, choose some fabrics that have a touch of gold or silver in the print, plus multi-colored prints, bright solids, and blacks. For a party or holiday jacket, use lamé or other dressmaking fabrics. Select silkier trim with a finer texture than you might choose to mix with denim and consider trims in gold or silver as well.

2. At the fabric store, pull fabrics that match the effect you wish to create. Evaluate your selections. Is there an overall color pattern or theme? Stack the bolts of fabrics, then stand back to look at your selections. If there isn't a dominant fabric that contains many of the colors you've chosen in the other fabrics, look for one to use as the main fabric in your jacket.

3. Add fabrics until you have the number required. For visual interest, try to include a large print, a solid, or two small, tone-on-tone prints that look like a solid from a distance, small and medium florals or geometric prints, and a stripe or a print with a definite pattern line to follow.

4. Arrange fabrics with like colors together so they blend in a gradual transition; evaluate. Does color flow smoothly from one fabric to the next? Remove any that stick out like a sore thumb—those that are too bright, too dull, too light, too dark. Substitute one that makes a smoother transition.

5. When you are pleased with your fabric selections, purchase the required yardage of each. Plan to use the fabric you love the most for those parts of the jacket that require the most yardage.

You can do this! Don't forget that you can add other fabrics later if something just doesn't work the way you thought it would!

✓ *Jacket Care*

If you must clean your finished jacket, be sure to ask the dry cleaner to clean and steam only. Pressing can ruin the beautiful patchwork and textures you've so carefully created on the surface of your jacket. If you are careful to spot clean your jacket whenever necessary, you can keep dry cleaning to a minimum.

✓ *Jacket Construction—General Directions*

♪ **NOTE:** In the illustrations that follow, the general shape of Jacket Eight will be illustrated—without the patchwork pieces. Basic construction steps are the same for the other four jacket styles.

1. The pullout pattern in this book includes the cutting lines for five different jacket styles in five different sizes. Determine which size pattern to use. Trace the appropriately sized pattern pieces for the jacket you are making onto pattern tracing paper or cloth.

2. Cut two sleeves, two fronts, and one back from the lining and foundation fabrics.

♪ **NOTE:** Pressing during the whole process of making the patchwork pieces and construction of the jacket is important. Don't skip pressing.

3. For Jacket Six only, stitch the foundation fronts to the foundation back at the shoulder before applying the patchwork pieces. Use $1/2$"-wide seam allowances. For Jacket Nine, stitch the left front only to the back at the shoulder before attaching the patchwork pieces. Press seams open. On Jackets Seven, Eight, and Ten, sew the fronts to the back at the shoulders *after* you have applied the patchwork pieces to the back. On all five jackets, attach the

sleeves *after* you have applied the patchwork pieces, following the directions in steps 10 and 11, on page 17.

4. Make the patchwork pieces for the jacket, *using $^1/_4$"-wide seam allowances* to sew the pieces together. In some cases this is very important, so be sure your machine is correctly marked for an accurate $^1/_4$"-wide seam or use a special quilting presser foot as a guide.

5. Lay the foundation flat with the right side facing up. Place the patchwork pieces on the foundation, following the specific instructions for the jacket you are making. Each time you add a new piece, smooth out any wrinkles and pin flat. Trim each piece to fit next to the other patchwork pieces and/or even with the outside edges of the foundation. Pin securely.

6. If you wish to add piping to the edge(s) of a completed patchwork piece, allow $^1/_4$" extra at each edge when trimming excess. Stitch the cording to the right side of the piece, then turn the seam to the wrong side and press. Use a piping foot or your zipper foot so you can stitch close to the corded edge through the foundation.

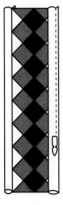

Use zipper foot
to stitch piping in place.

If you are using gimp or braid to cover the raw edges of the patchwork pieces, just butt the edges of the adjoining patchwork pieces together. Then zigzag over the raw edges through the foundation to hold them in place on the jacket foundation.

Center braid or gimp over the raw edges. If using gimp, zigzag both edges in place. The piping foot works well for attaching some types of gimp. If covering raw edges with a flat braid or binding, straight-stitch along both edges of the trim.

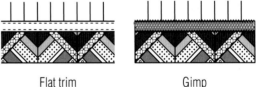

Flat trim   Gimp

Trim the outer edges of the patchwork pieces even with the foundation and stitch in place $^1/_4$" from the raw edges.

7. Cut and apply fusible interfacing to the jacket fronts and back neckline (or to the facings) as directed in the specific preparation and finishing directions for each jacket.

8. When the jacket foundation is completely covered, sew the fronts to the back at the shoulders and press the seams open (if you have not already done so when following specific jacket instructions). Cover the shoulder seams of the patchwork jacket with trim as desired. With right sides together, sew the lining fronts to the lining back.

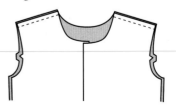

9. Place the completed jacket body and lining wrong sides together. Do the same thing with the jacket and lining sleeves. Since there is so much stitching to hold the patchwork pieces in place, the jacket body and sleeves may now be a little smaller than the lining. Trim any excess lining even with the raw edges of the jacket and sleeves.

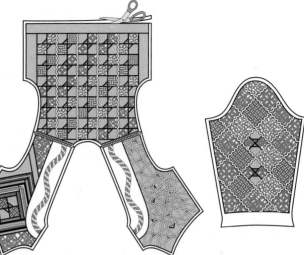

10. Machine baste from dot to dot along the seam line on each jacket and lining sleeve cap.

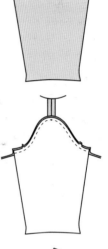

11. Pin the sleeves to the jacket armholes, matching notches and the center dot to the shoulder seam line. Draw up the basting stitches to fit. Adjust gathers evenly. Stitch. Remove the basting.

12. Press the seam toward the sleeve. On the right side, cover the sleeve seam lines with trim if desired. Sew the lining sleeves to the jacket lining, drawing up the basting stitches to fit. Press the seams toward the sleeves.
13. With the jacket right sides together, stitch the side seams, continuing to the bottom edge of the sleeve. Repeat with the lining.

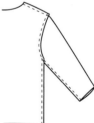

14. Carefully steam-press the completed jacket, being careful not to smash or rearrange any of the textures you have worked to create.
15. Pin the shoulder pads inside the jacket, try on, and adjust as necessary. Sew the shoulder pads to the shoulder seam by hand and loosely hand-tack the corners to the armhole seam allowance.
16. Follow the specific instructions for lining and finishing each jacket.
17. Get ready for the compliments!
18. Start your next jacket!

Tack to jacket foundation.

Handtack to seam allowance.

JACKET · SIX
Kaleidoscope Twist

◆ **Kaleidoscope Radiance**

◆ **Woven Patch Closure**

◆ **Pleated Perfection**

◆ **Strip-Pieced Triangles**

◆ **Strip-Stitched Scrappys**

◆ **Fused Fragments**

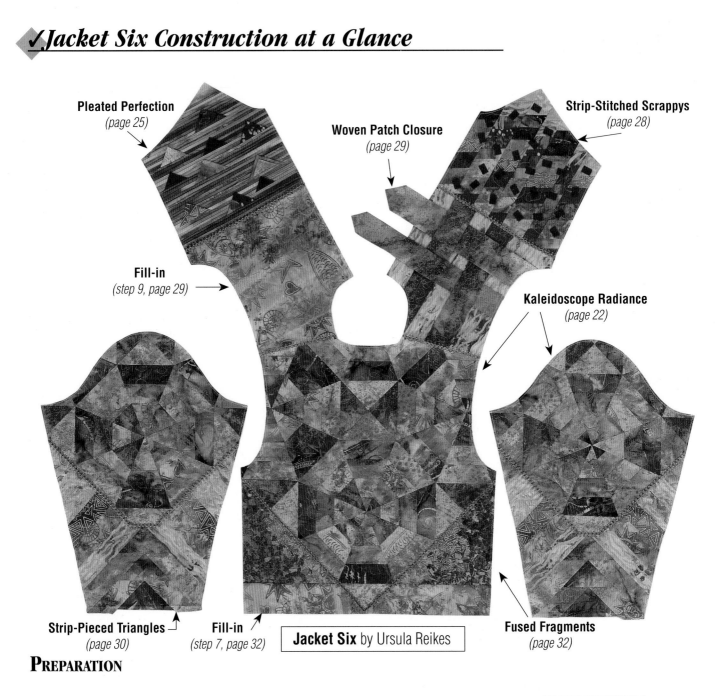

Pleated Perfection
(page 25)

Woven Patch Closure
(page 29)

Strip-Stitched Scrappys
(page 28)

Fill-in
(step 9, page 29)

Kaleidoscope Radiance
(page 22)

Strip-Pieced Triangles ⌐
(page 30)

Fill-in
(step 7, page 32)

Jacket Six by Ursula Reikes

Fused Fragments
(page 32)

PREPARATION

1. Cut the jacket fronts, back, and sleeves from the muslin or flannel foundation fabric and from the lining fabric. Set the lining pieces aside.
2. Sew the jacket front foundation pieces to the jacket back at the shoulder seams and press the seams open.
3. Place the foundation on a flat surface and draw a line on each foundation front 2" below the shoulder seam line. The Kaleidoscope Radiance patchwork on the jacket back will come forward to this line. If you prefer, you may place the Kaleidoscope on the back only as shown in the jacket on this page. One reason for bringing the patchwork from the back forward to the front is to unify the front and back. If your fabric choices are well integrated, as in the jacket shown above, this may not be necessary.

2" below
shoulder seam

Shopping List

All yardage requirements are based on 44"-wide fabrics, unless otherwise noted. When using the same fabric for more than one patchwork technique, combine the yardage requirements.

Jacket Foundation	2 yds. cotton flannel or muslin*
Jacket Lining	2 yds. silky lining fabric or smooth cotton fabric
Interfacing	3/8 yd. lightweight fusible interfacing
Shoulder Pads	Raglan-style shoulder pads (3/8" to 3/4" thick)
Kaleidoscope Radiance	2/3 yd. each of 4 different fabrics that coordinate with the theme fabric for Pleated Perfection (below) Fabric #1: Very Dark Fabric #2: Medium Dark Fabric #3: Medium Light Fabric #4: Contrast
Pleated Perfection	1 yd. fabric (See Fabric Selection Tips, below.) Fabrics #3 and #4 above (or other contrasting fabric of your choice) for points
Strip-Stitched Scrappys	Strips left over from any of the above fabrics
Woven Patch Closure	1/3 yd. each of 3 or 4 high-contrast fabrics the same as or different than Fabrics #1, #2, #3, and #4 for Kaleidoscope Radiance
Strip-Pieced Triangles	Leftovers from other techniques or 2/3 yd. if you prefer to cut all strips from the same fabric. You can also use this fabric for the background behind the tabs on the left front.
Fused Fragments	Snips from fabric leftovers 12" x 12" square of background fabric 12" x 12" square of Fine Fuse and a Teflon press cloth Hot Stitch Glue Powder by Aleene Metallic machine embroidery thread
Decorative Trim	Approximately 4 yds. of braid or piping
Buttons	5 or 6 buttons, 1/2" diameter
Snaps	2, for upper jacket front

Preshrink the foundation fabric, allow to dry, and press to remove wrinkles.

In addition to the fabrics and notions listed, you will need the following special supplies:

Knife Pleater (EZE PLEATER or Perfect Pleater)
45° Kaleidoscope Wedge Ruler by Omnigrid®
ScrapMaster (formerly ScrapSaver) cutting guide by That Patchwork Place
or 5" x 5" square of plastic template material

FABRIC SELECTION TIPS

- First, choose a theme print for the Pleated Perfection and then choose the remaining fabrics to coordinate with it.
- For Fabric #4 in Kaleidoscope Radiance, select white, cream, black, or another color that is a definite contrast from the other three fabrics. If you prefer low contrast in the Kaleidoscope, study the fabric choices in the jacket shown on page 20.
- Make a swatch card to identify your fabrics to avoid confusion later. Make sure you have the following:
  Theme Print
  Background
  Fabric #1: Very Dark
  Fabric #2: Medium Dark
  Fabric #3: Medium Light
  Fabric #4: Contrast
  Fabrics #5, #6, and #7: same as Fabrics #1, #2, and #3 or 1/3 yd. each of 3 to 4 different fabrics

✓ *Kaleidoscope Radiance*

MATERIALS

²/₃ yd. each of 4 different fabrics that coordinate with
the theme fabric for Pleated Perfection:
      Fabric #1: Very Dark
      Fabric #2: Medium Dark
      Fabric #3: Medium Light
      Fabric #4: Contrast

DIRECTIONS

*Cut all strips across the width of the fabric from selvage
to selvage.*

1. From each of the 4 fabrics, cut 6 strips, each 2" wide.
    You will have a total of 24 strips.
2. From Fabric #2 and from Fabric #3, cut 8 squares,
    each 4¹/₂" x 4¹/₂", for a total of 16 squares. Stack the
    squares in groups of 3 or 4 and cut once diagonally
    for a total of 32 triangles to use for the corners in
    Blocks A and B. Set aside for step 9 on page 23.

Cut 32.

3. Using 24 of the strips cut in step 1, make 6 identical
    strip-pieced units. Arrange the strips in numerical
    order and stitch together ¹/₄" from the long edges.
    Press all seams toward the darkest strip. Each unit
    should measure approximately 6¹/₂" x 42".

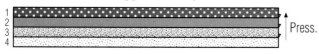

Make 6.

4. Use the 6¹/₂" marking on the 45° Kaleidoscope Wedge
    Ruler to cut 14 to 15 wedges from each of the strips.
    Cut with the wedge point up and then with the point
    down, alternating until you can no longer cut a
    triangle from the strip unit. You will need a total of

72* wedges for this project. Save one strip-pieced unit
for Strip-Stitched Scrappys on page 28.

As you position the ruler and cut, make sure the
seam lines are parallel to the horizontal lines on the
ruler.

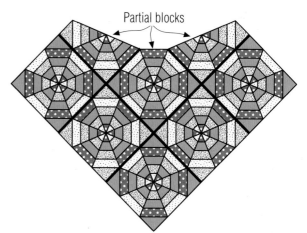

♪ **NOTE:** If the fabric seams are not running parallel to the ruler lines, adjust the ruler and make a
small cut in your fabric to re-establish the perfect
wedge. Keep any slivers left over from this for the
Fused Fragments technique on page 32.

*If you follow these directions, you will have a
completed piece of patchwork that will be more than
large enough for the jacket back and front shoulder
area. You will have leftover patchwork to use in another jacket or a vest like the one shown on page 106.
If you prefer, you can make just enough blocks and
partial blocks to cover the foundation with little left
over. The number needed will depend on the size you
are making; the patchwork piece will probably look
like the illustration below.*

Partial blocks

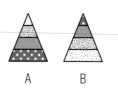

5. Divide the wedges into 2 stacks, placing those with
    Fabric #1 at the wide end in Stack A (dark wedges)
    and those with Fabric #4 at the wide end in Stack B
    (light wedges).

A   B

6. Sew the light and dark wedges together in pairs, chain sewing to make quick work of it. Always place the light wedge on the bottom and the dark wedge on top with right sides together and seam lines matching. Because you pressed all seams toward the darkest strip in each strip unit, the seams should butt for a perfect match, eliminating the need for much pinning. Stitch from the wide end to the point; press seam toward dark wedge.

🎵 **NOTE:** Chain piecing saves time and thread. Instead of stopping the machine, lifting the presser foot, and cutting the thread after sewing two pieces together, place another pair just in front of the previous pair and continue stitching. Clip the pairs apart, then chain-sew the pairs together in groups of four in the same manner.

7. Sew the pairs together to create half-blocks in the same manner. Press all seams in the same direction. Trim points that extend beyond the outer edge of the half-blocks and save for Fused Fragments, page 32.

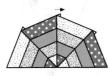

8. Sew the half-blocks together in pairs to create 9 octagonal blocks, making sure that the seams match at the center and that the outer ends of the wedges match. Stitch from the center out, then flip the piece over and stitch from the center to the opposite end. Press seams in the same direction as all other seams. There will be a slight twist in the center. Press each block flat from the right side.

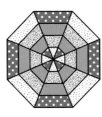

Make 9.

9. Divide the blocks into 2 stacks of 4 blocks each and set the 1 remaining block aside. Rotate the first stack so that the dark-ended wedges are at the center on all 4 sides as shown for Block A. Add a dark triangle (cut in step 2) to the 4 light-wedge ends of each octagon to create square blocks. Position the second stack of blocks so the light-ended wedges are at the center on all 4 sides and sew *light* triangles to the dark corner wedges as shown for Block B.

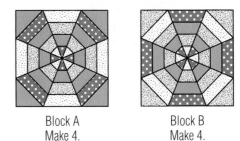

Block A
Make 4.

Block B
Make 4.

🎵 **NOTE:** If you make another piece of Kaleidoscope Radiance patchwork for another jacket or vest, consider using two different medium value fabrics for the corners instead of light and dark for a different look.

10. Before you sew the completed blocks together to complete the patchwork piece, decide whether you want dark or light points at the bottom of the jacket back and on the sleeves. For a jacket with light corners, sew the triangles from Fabric #3 (step 2, page 22) to the dark wedge ends of the remaining block.

    For a jacket with dark corners, sew the triangles from Fabric #2 (step 2, page 22) to the light wedge ends of the remaining block.

11. Arrange the blocks into 3 rows of 3 blocks each, alternating Blocks A and B.

🎵 **NOTE:** Three of the four corner-blocks of the finished piece of patchwork will show on your jacket (back and sleeves.) Place your best piecing in these locations.

12. Sew the blocks together in rows, matching seams and pinning to secure for stitching. Press the seams in opposite directions row to row. Then sew the rows

together, matching seams carefully. Press the seams in one direction, then press the completed piece of patchwork smooth and flat.

For jackets with dark corners

For jackets with light corners

♪ **NOTE:** This design was adapted with permission from Marilyn Doheny's Cutting Edge Quilt Designs as found on the Kaleidoscope Ruler package.

13. Lay the jacket foundation on a flat surface. Place 1 corner of the completed Kaleidoscope Radiance on the foundation back even with the bottom of the jacket. When the jacket hem is turned up, the point will extend below it. The other 3 corners will extend beyond the foundation. Pin securely in place, making sure that the patchwork is accurately centered on the jacket back. Carefully turn the pieces over and smooth out on a flat surface.

14. Cut the patchwork away along the back at the sides and around the armhole edges, ending at the lines you drew on the foundation fronts 2" below the front

shoulders (step 3 of "Preparation," page 20). Turn the foundation fronts back along the lines and continue cutting the patchwork along the folded edges of the foundation, the upper front neckline edges, and the back neckline. The goal is to end up with only two pieces of patchwork, one that is pinned to the foundation and a large piece to set aside for the sleeves.

Stitch patchwork to foundation ¼" from the raw edges of the armhole and neckline edges only.

15. Fold each foundation sleeve in half at the shoulder dot and press a crease. Do the same with the paper pattern. Place the sleeves on a flat surface and make sure you have them positioned so you have a right and left sleeve.

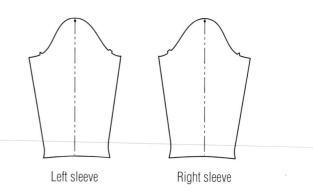

Left sleeve   Right sleeve

16. Place the sleeve pattern piece face up on the right side of 1 of the remaining patchwork points (where you cut the armhole edges). Center the crease line over the center of the Kaleidoscope design, and position so that you can utilize as much of the patchwork as possible on the sleeve. Pin in place and cut out 1 sleeve.

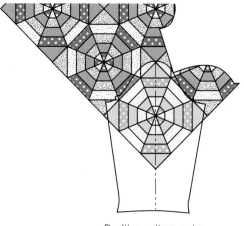

Position pattern on top of Kaleidoscope leftover.

17. Remove the pattern piece from the patchwork sleeve. Place the patchwork sleeve right side down on the right side of the opposite patchwork point and adjust so that the pattern matches exactly. Pin in place; cut second sleeve.
18. Position a patchwork piece on each foundation sleeve with the centers of the Kaleidoscope designs matching the creases in the sleeves. Be sure to match front and back armhole notches. Pin in place; stitch ¹⁄₄" from the underarm and sleeve-cap edges only.

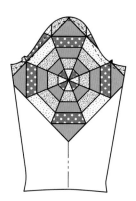

✓Pleated Perfection

MATERIALS

1 yd. theme fabric
Scraps of other fabrics used in jacket
³⁄₈ yd. lightweight fusible interfacing

DIRECTIONS

You will need the Perfect Pleater or EZE PLEATER designed to make ¹⁄₄"-deep pleats. A pleater has stiff, permanent pleats (or tucks), called "louvers" in the following directions.

1. Cut a piece of fusible interfacing for the left front, cutting up to the armhole level along the side and front edges. The fusible adhesive (rough) side of the interfacing must face up. Set aside for step 4, below.

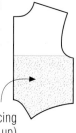

Fusible interfacing (adhesive side up)

2. Place the pleater on the ironing board with the louver edges facing away from you.
3. Position the 1-yard piece of theme fabric *wrong side up* on top of the pleater with 1 corner 3" from the lower right corner of the pleater as shown. This will be the front bottom point of your jacket left front and you will be pleating the fabric on the bias.

4. Firmly tuck the fabric into each louver, beginning with the one closest to you. Use a very thin metal or

plastic ruler or a credit card to push the fabric completely into each louver before making the next pleat. Work from the center out on each row.

As you make the first tuck, make sure the bottom point of the fabric does not pull up out of position. Use your other hand to hold it in place.

Repeat the tucking process until you have made 5 to 8 pleats. Steam press these in place, pressing pleats in position beyond the outer edges of the pleater if necessary to make a pleated piece wide enough to cover the jacket foundation from the front edge to the side-seam edge. (The pleater may not be as wide as your fabric or jacket front.)

5. To hold these first few pleats in place before removing the fabric from the pleater, *apply the lower portion only* of the left front fusible interfacing (cut in step 1) to the wrong side of the pleated fabric. Begin by placing the lower corner of the fusible in the corner where you started making the pleats. The fusible adhesive should be facing the fabric.

Be sure to follow the manufacturer's directions for fusing, using adequate steam and pressure for a permanent fuse. Allow the fabric to cool and then roll the pleater away from the fabric to remove it.

6. Continue pleating, pressing, and applying the interfacing in 5- to 8-pleat increments, until you have pleated enough fabric to cover the foundation. (Use the interfacing as a guide.) Remove from the pleater and trim the pleated fabric even with the edges of the interfacing.

NOTE: To continue the pleats, fold the already-pleated fabric and the interfacing away from the pleater and lay the last pleat into the first row of tucks in the pleater.

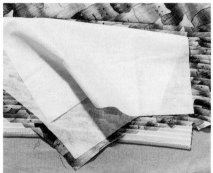

7. Place the pleated fabric in position on top of the left front foundation and pin in place. Stitch ¼" from the raw edges.

8. Place the jacket pattern piece on top of the left front and draw a line along the top edge of the Pleated Perfection. Set it aside for step 5 in Strip-Stitched Scrappys, page 28.

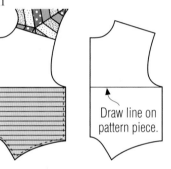

Draw line on pattern piece.

9. Cover the upper left front foundation fabric with a fabric that will contrast with the fabric you plan to use for the tabs on the upper right front. Cut a rectangle of fabric, larger than the section to be covered, and place the short edge right sides together with the upper edge of the pleated fabric.

Stitch ¼" from the raw edges, then flip the fabric up to cover the foundation. Trim even with the foundation edges and the bottom edge of the Kaleidoscope patchwork. Stitch ¼" from all raw edges. Cover the lower seam and the place where the fabric meets the Kaleidoscope with braid or cording.

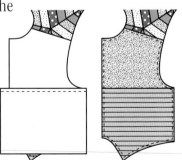

10. Make 9 or 10 points to embellish the pleats, using one of the two methods shown below. Use one or more different fabrics as desired.

11. Arrange the points on the pleated fabric as desired, then tuck the raw edge of each one into the pleat. With contrasting thread (and a decorative stitch if desired), stitch through the center of each pleat that has a point, making sure that you catch the point in the stitching. Be sure to leave points free of stitching in tucks that lie beneath them.

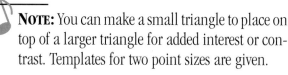

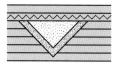**NOTE:** You can make a small triangle to place on top of a larger triangle for added interest or contrast. Templates for two point sizes are given.

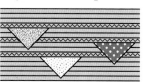

Stack points for added interest.

Method 1

1. Using the ScrapMaster cutting guide, cut $3^7/8$" triangles from the chosen fabrics. If you prefer, make a plastic template for cutting triangles, using the printed template below right.

2. Fold each triangle in half and stitch $^1/4$" from the shortest side. Clip corners, turn right side out; press.

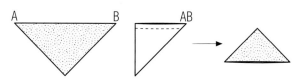

Method 2

1. For every 2 triangles, cut 2 squares, each $1^7/8$" or $2^3/8$" square. Use the ScrapMaster cutting guide (or plastic templates made from those given above right) and cut the squares from 2 different fabrics.

2. Place the squares right sides together and stitch $^1/4$" from all raw edges.

3. Cut the stitched square once diagonally to make 2 triangles. Clip the corner, turn right side out; press.

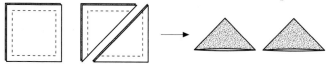

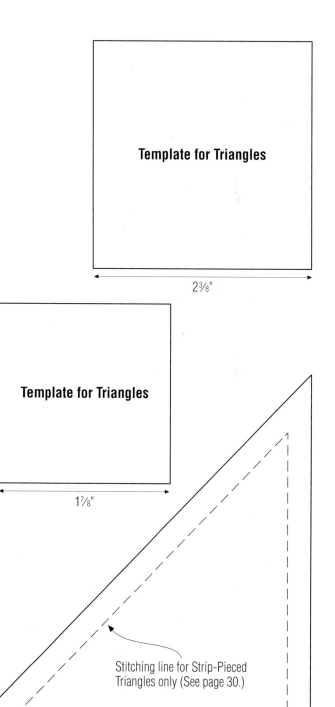

Template for Triangles

$2^3/8$"

Template for Triangles

$1^7/8$"

Stitching line for Strip-Pieced Triangles only (See page 30.)

$3^7/8$"

✓Strip-Stitched Scrappys

MATERIALS

Leftover fabrics from other techniques, including the leftover strip-pieced unit from Kaleidoscope Radiance

Decorative thread or Ribbon Floss for the bobbin

DIRECTIONS

1. Fold the 6½"-wide strip-pieced unit from Kaleidoscope Radiance in half crosswise and cut into 2 pieces of equal length.

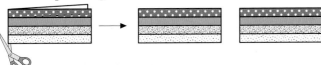

2. Cut an assortment of 1"- to 2"-wide fabric strips that are the same length as the 2 strip-pieced units. Arrange the strip-pieced units one above the other and add the assorted strips between, above, and below the units so contrasting fabrics are next to each other. Sew the strips together to make a strip-pieced unit 20" wide. Press all seams in one direction.

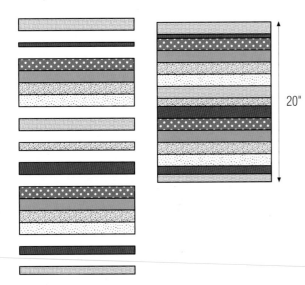

20"

3. Place the 60° line on a 24"-long ruler even with the top edge of the strip-pieced unit. Make a 60° cut. Using the cut edge as a guide, cut the unit into strips, varying the width from 1" to no more than 3".

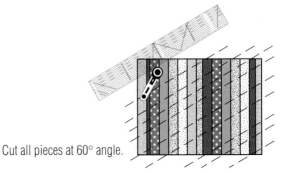

Cut all pieces at 60° angle.

4. Arrange the strips next to each other, offsetting them and turning some around to create a new design. When pleased with the results, stitch the strips together, using ¼"-wide seams. You will need a piece large enough to cover the same area on the right front foundation that you covered with Pleated Perfection on the left front.

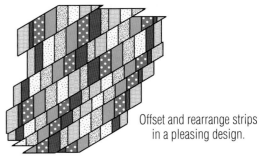

Offset and rearrange strips in a pleasing design.

5. Place the jacket front pattern piece on top of the completed patchwork, positioning it as desired and being sure it is positioned for a right front. Fold the pattern piece down along the line you drew earlier. (See step 8 in Pleated Perfection on page 26.) Pin the pattern in place and cut out the lower section for the lower right front.

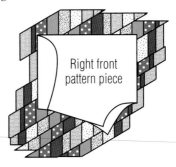

Right front pattern piece

6. Position the completed patchwork on the right front foundation, pin in place, and stitch ¼" from the raw edges along the front, bottom, and side.

7. Cut a ¾"-wide strip of fabric that will show up against the patchwork on the lower right front. From this strip, cut scraps of varying widths, none wider than ½". Cut approximately 30 Scrappys.

8. Position the Scrappys on top of the patchwork in the desired pattern. Machine stitch across them to hold them in place. Use a decorative thread in your sewing machine.

If you would like to experiment with Ribbon Floss, hand wind it onto a bobbin. When you thread your machine, bypass the tension in the bobbin case if your machine has a drop-in bobbin. If your machine has a bobbin case, purchase an extra bobbin case and loosen the tension screw so the Ribbon Floss slides through easily. Stitch with the foundation side up. You will be stitching "blind" so you will have to use the pins holding the Scrappys in place as a guide. Do a test first to see if you like the results. Experiment with different kinds of stitches.

9. Cover the upper right front with the fabric of your choice, following step 9 for Pleated Perfection on page 27. Do not cover the top edge with trim yet.

✓Woven Patch Closure

MATERIALS

⅓ yd. each of 3 or 4 high-contrast fabrics the same as or different than Fabrics #1, #2, #3, and #4 for Kaleidoscope Radiance

5 or 6 buttons, ½" diameter

DIRECTIONS

1. Select 2 different fabrics for the tabbed closures. Cut 1 piece 5" wide and long enough to cross over to the left front (approximately 14" to 15" long) for the upper tab. For the lower tab, cut a piece 6" wide and long enough to cross over. You can make the tabs the same length or different lengths.

2. Fold each strip in half lengthwise with right sides together and cut a point at one end as shown. Stitch ¼" from the long raw edges and point. Clip the corners, turn right side out, and press.

3. Position the finished tabs across the right front in the desired location, leaving at least 1" of space between them. Pin in place at the armhole, then stitch ¼" from the raw edges.

Position tabs and stitch in place at armhole edge.

4. For the weaving strips, cut 2 to 4 strips of fabric long enough to reach from the Kaleidoscope patchwork to the top edge of the Strip-Stitched Scrappys. You may

vary the strip width from $2\frac{1}{2}$" to 5". Fold each strip in half lengthwise with right sides together and stitch $\frac{1}{4}$" from the long raw edges. Turn right side out and press.

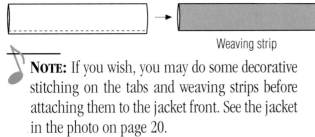

Weaving strip

♪ **NOTE:** If you wish, you may do some decorative stitching on the tabs and weaving strips before attaching them to the jacket front. See the jacket in the photo on page 20.

5. Weave the finished strips in and out of the tabs, leaving some of the upper front fabric showing in between strips. Pin in place. Stitch the top and bottom ends of the weaving strips in place $\frac{1}{8}$" from the raw edges. Cover the raw edges of the strips and Kaleidoscope patchwork with braid or cording. Do the same at the bottom edges of the weaving strips.

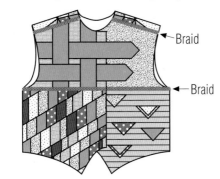

Braid

Braid

♪ **NOTE:** If you would rather wear your jacket open, you can do weaving on both jacket fronts with the horizontal strips ending at each front edge.

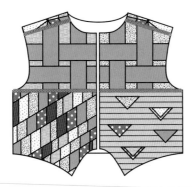

✓ *Strip-Pieced Triangles*

MATERIALS

Leftovers from other patchwork techniques or $\frac{2}{3}$ yd. if you prefer to cut all strips from the same fabric

Scraps of fabric for triangles, which should contrast with the fabric(s) used for the strips

DIRECTIONS

1. Using the ScrapMaster cutting guide or a template made from the one on page 27, cut 4 triangles, each $3\frac{7}{8}$", for each sleeve. (Smaller sizes may require only 3 triangles for each sleeve; larger sizes may require additional triangles.) Mark the $\frac{1}{4}$" seam-line intersections on the right side of each triangle as shown.

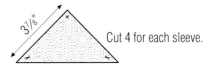

Cut 4 for each sleeve.

2. From the fabric leftovers, cut several strips of fabric, each 2" wide.

3. To make a marking template for the triangle positions, trace the $3\frac{7}{8}$" triangle on page 27 onto template plastic. Cut out carefully.

4. Position the marking template on the sleeve foundation with the point lined up with the bottom point of the Kaleidoscope piece (on the center crease you pressed earlier). Use a sharp lead pencil to trace around the triangle onto the foundation.

   Continue positioning the template and marking around it until you reach the bottom of the sleeve. Depending on the position of the Kaleidoscope and the length of the sleeve, the last triangle may only be a partial one.

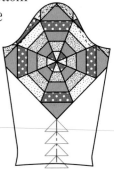

5. Pin a triangle *in the bottom position* with the $1/4$" seam line marks matching the traced triangle lines underneath. When correctly positioned, the top point of the triangle will overlap the bottom line for the triangle above it. If the bottom edge of the triangle extends below the bottom edge of the sleeve, trim away the excess.

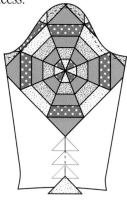

Position first triangle.

6. With right sides together, stitch a 2"-wide strip of fabric to each side of the triangle. Turn the strip toward the foundation and press. Pin in place and trim the strips even with the outer edges of the foundation. Place the $1/4$" mark of a ruler at the point of the triangle and draw a line across the strips parallel to the lower edge of the sleeve. Remove the ruler and trim away excess on each strip.

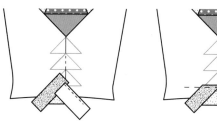 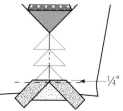

7. With right sides together, pin the long edge of the next triangle to the top edge of the cut strips. Stitch $1/4$" from the raw edges. Turn the triangle up to make sure you didn't stitch across the triangle point. If you did, stitch a narrower seam and remove the first stitching.

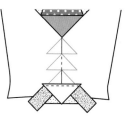

Turn the triangle up onto the foundation and press. Add strips, press, and trim as before.

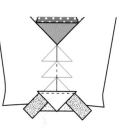

Continue this process until you have added all triangles, then continue adding parallel strips until the foundation is covered. Trim strip ends even with the foundation and the Kaleidoscope patchwork. Cover the raw edges of the Kaleidoscope with the trim of your choice.

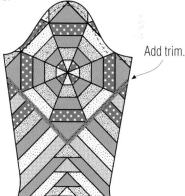

Add trim.

◆✓*Fused Fragments*

MATERIALS

Fabric leftovers
12" x 12" square of background fabric
12" x 12" square of Fine Fuse and a Teflon press cloth*
Hot Stitch Glue Powder by Aleene
Metallic machine-embroidery thread (or other
   contrasting thread of your choice)

*If this is not available in your area, substitute a
square of paper-backed fusible web, such as Wonder-
Under. After applying to the fabric (step 1, below),
remove the backing paper carefully and save the
paper to use in place of the Teflon press cloth. Fine
Fuse seems to work better.*

DIRECTIONS

1. Apply Fine Fuse to the *right side* of the 12" square of
   background fabric, following the manufacturer's directions. Allow to cool, then remove the paper backing if using paper-backed fusible web.
2. Cut snips from fabric leftovers into confetti fragments
   using a rotary cutter and mat.
3. Place a thin layer of fragments on the *right side* of
   background square. Mix them up, or place fragments
   of each fabric in
   individual areas.
   Shake and mix
   glue powder in
   with fragments.

4. Cover the fragments with the Teflon press cloth (or
   the release paper from the Wonder-Under) and press
   with a hot iron. Carefully remove the sheet from the

fragments. You may need to scrape some snips off of
the pressing sheet, replace them on the background
fabric square, and press again with the press cloth.

5. Stitch all over
   the fragments;
   cut the square
   once diagonally
   to make two tri-
   angles.

6. Position a triangle in each lower corner on the
   jacket back foundation, with the long edge
   next to the Kaleidoscope. Pin in place, then
   trim the triangles even with the sides of
   the foundation. Cut the triangles
   along the bottom edge so that
   they extend ¼" below the
   back hemline. Pin to
   foundation.

Add more stitching if necessary to securely anchor the fragments or for further embellishment.

7. Cut a strip of fabric ½" wider than the hem allowance. Fold the Kaleidoscope point up out of the way
   and, with right sides together, stitch the strip to the
   bottom edge of the Fused Fragment triangles ¼"
   from the edge (along the back hemline). Turn the
   strip down and trim even with the bottom edge of the
   foundation.

Kaleidoscope point turned back

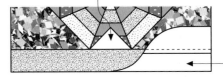

Jacket foundation
hem allowance

✓ Jacket Finishing

1. To finish the Kaleidoscope point at the bottom edge of the jacket back, cut a $3^7/8"$ triangle using the ScrapMaster or the template on page 27.

2. Turn the jacket back hem up and out of the way. Pin the remaining triangle to the point, with right sides together and raw edges even. Being careful not to catch the jacket back or hem allowance, stitch $1/4"$ from the raw edges of the point, clip the corner, turn right side out, and press. Trim the finished point with braid or cording as desired.

Stitch triangle facing to point.

3. Turn under $1/4"$ on the lower edge of the jacket back and press. Edgestitch, being careful not to catch the Kaleidoscope point in the stitching.

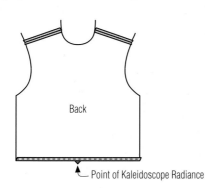

Back

Point of Kaleidoscope Radiance

4. Cut facings from a coordinating fabric and from lightweight fusible interfacing. Apply interfacing to the wrong side of the facings, following the manufacturer's directions.

5. With right sides together, stitch the back neck facing to the front facings at the shoulder, trim seams to $1/4"$, and press them open. Finish the outer edges of the facings with zigzagging or serging, or turn under $1/4"$, press, and edgestitch.

6. Compare the completed patchwork jacket and sleeves to the corresponding lining pieces as shown in step 9 on page 17.

7. Trim away $1^1/4"$ at the lower edge of the jacket back lining and at the lower edge of each sleeve lining.

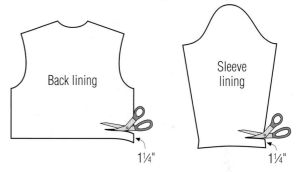

Back lining

Sleeve lining

$1^1/4"$ $1^1/4"$

8. Prepare and sew the patchwork sleeves to the jacket and the lining sleeves to the lining as shown in steps 10–12 on page 17.

9. With right sides together, stitch the lining front to the back, matching underarm seams. Press the seams open.

   With right sides together, stitch the jacket side seams, ending the stitching $1/2"$ from the bottom edge of the jacket front. The bottom edge of the jacket back should extend 1" below the bottom edge of the jacket front.

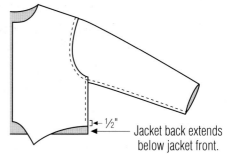

$1/2"$ Jacket back extends below jacket front.

10. Complete step 14 on page 17. Sew the shoulder pads in place as shown in step 15 on page 17.

11. Place the lining and jacket with *wrong sides together* and raw edges even. Stitch ¼" from the raw edges.

12. With right sides together, stitch the facing to the jacket along the back neckline, front neckline, and bottom edges. Trim the seam to ¼", clip corners, and turn the facing to the inside. Press.

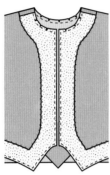

13. Understitch (machine-stitch close to the seamline) the remaining seam allowance to the facing around the neckline, front, and bottom edges.

14. Turn up the bottom edge of the jacket back along the hemline. Press. Slipstitch in place. Turn the front facing up, turning under the side seam allowance. Slipstitch in place.

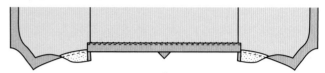

15. Hem the jacket sleeves over the lining.

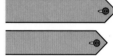

16. Make buttonholes in the right jacket front at the locations marked on the pattern for Jacket 6. Sew buttons in place. Make a horizontal buttonhole at the end of each tab. Sew buttons to left front in position under the tabs. Sew snaps in place on upper jacket fronts.

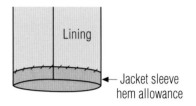

Jacket Six by Judy Murrah, Victoria, Texas. Gold accents on buttons and trim add pizzazz to this study in pinks and purples.

Jacket Six by Michelle Goodson, Victoria, Texas. Ending the tabs at the center front edge leaves the upper left front free for additional embellishment.

Kaleidoscope Twist **35**

Boogie Bargello

 Tricky Triangles

 Boogie Bargello

 Overlapping Flaps

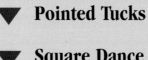 **Pointed Tucks**

 Square Dance

 Tasseled Triangles

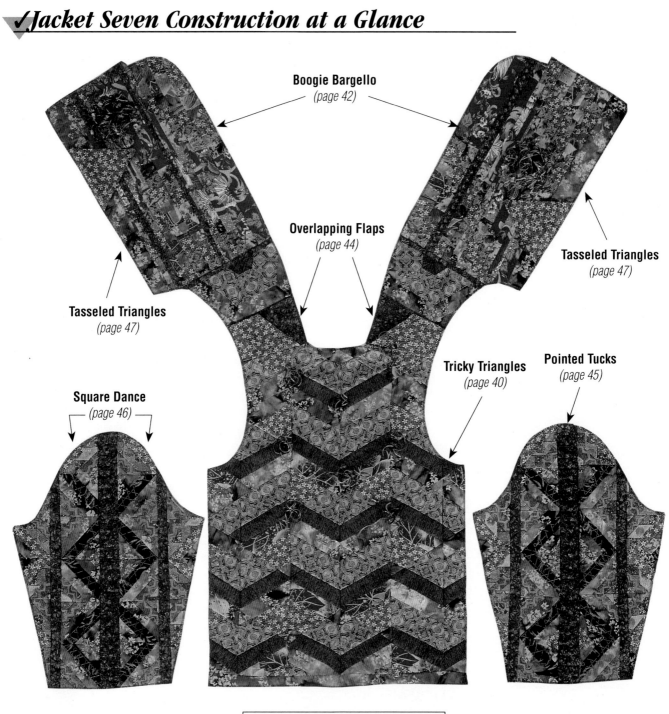

Boogie Bargello
(page 42)

Overlapping Flaps
(page 44)

Tasseled Triangles
(page 47)

Tasseled Triangles
(page 47)

Pointed Tucks
(page 45)

Tricky Triangles
(page 40)

Square Dance
(page 46)

Jacket Seven by Susan I. Jones

PREPARATION

1. Cut the jacket back, fronts, and sleeves from the foundation fabric and from the lining. Cut lightweight fusible interfacing, using the front and back neckline facing pattern pieces for Jacket Seven. Set the lining pieces aside.

2. Following the manufacturer's directions, apply the fusible interfacing to the wrong side of the jacket front and back foundation pieces.

Shopping List

All yardage requirements are based on 44"-wide fabrics, unless otherwise noted. When using the same fabric for more than one patchwork technique, combine the yardage requirements.

Jacket Foundation	3 yds. cotton flannel or muslin*	
Jacket Lining	3 yds. silky lining fabric or smooth cotton fabric	
Interfacing	1/2 yd. lightweight fusible interfacing	
Shoulder Pads	Raglan-style shoulder pads (3/8" to 3/4" thick)	
Tricky Triangles	Color Family 1 (Background color)	Color Family 2 (Accent color)
	1/3 yd. Dark	1/8 yd. Dark
	1/2 yd. Medium	1/4 yd. Medium
	1/3 yd. Light	1/8 yd. Light
Boogie Bargello	1/3 yd. Light	1/8 yd. Dark
	1/8 yd. Dark	1/8 yd. Medium Dark
		1/16 yd. Medium
		1/8 yd. Medium Light
		1/16 yd. Light
Overlapping Flaps	1/4 yd. Medium Dark	
	1/4 yd. Medium Light	
Pointed Tucks		1/3 yd. Dark
Square Dance	1/4 yd. Medium Dark	1/4 yd. Medium Dark
	1/4 yd. Medium Light	1/4 yd. Medium
	1/4 yd. Light	1/4 yd. Medium Light
Thread (optional)	Perle cotton or other heavier thread for tying Tricky Triangles patchwork	
Decorative Trim	Approximately 5 yds. of braid or gimp	
Piping	5 yds. for finishing jacket and sleeve edges	
Tassels	2 small ones in same color as thread for tying**	
Buttons	3 buttons, 1" diameter, or 1 button, 2" diameter, for front closure	
	4 buttons, 1/2" diameter, for the overlapping flaps	
	2 buttons, 1/2" diameter, for Tasseled Triangles	
	36 to 38 small shank-style buttons or charms to embellish the Pointed Tucks	
	1 dozen assorted small buttons for "Boogie Bargello"	

*Preshrink the foundation fabric, allow to dry, and press to remove wrinkles.
**If tassels that match thread are unavailable, make your own tassels, using the tying thread or other assorted yarns and threads of your choice. See page 47.

In addition to the fabrics and notions listed, you will need the following special supplies:
   60° equilateral triangle ruler, at least 6" tall, to use with your rotary cutter
   Quilter's Rule™ Jr. (4 1/2" x 14") or other 4 1/2" ruler with a 45° line
   1 3/8" x 5" strip of sturdy cardboard

FABRIC SELECTION TIPS

- Choose two color families, then select fabrics in five different values from light to dark in each family. You need a total of ten fabrics. Remember that the lightest fabric in Color Family 1 will be the most pronounced fabric in the finished jacket.

- For easy reference, make a swatch card with a piece of each fabric glued to it and label each with the appropriate family number and value as listed below. Total yardage required is given with each fabric.

Color Family 1

Dark 1	1/2 yd.
Medium Dark 1	1/2 yd.
Medium 1	1/2 yd.
Medium Light 1	1/2 yd.
Light 1	1 yd.

Color Family 2

Dark 2	1/2 yd.
Medium Dark 2	1/3 yd.
Medium 2	1/2 yd.
Medium Light 2	1/3 yd.
Light 2	1/4 yd.

✓Tricky Triangles

MATERIALS

Color Family 1 (Background color)	Color Family 2 (Accent color)
¹/₃ yd. Dark	¹/₈ yd. Dark
¹/₂ yd. Medium	¹/₄ yd. Medium
¹/₃ yd. Light	¹/₈ yd. Light

DIRECTIONS

Cut all strips across the width of the fabric from selvage to selvage.

1. From Color Family 1, cut:
   5 strips of Dark, each 2" wide
   5 strips of Medium, each 3" wide
   5 strips of Light, each 2" wide
2. Make 5 identical strip-pieced units, arranging strips as shown. Sew strips together ¹/₄" from the long raw edges. Press the seams toward the darkest strip.

Color Family #1
Make 5 strip-pieced units.

3. From Color Family 2, cut:
   2 strips of Dark, each 2" wide
   2 strips of Medium, each 3" wide
   2 strips of Light, each 2" wide
4. Make 2 identical strip-pieced units, arranging the strips in each set in the same order as the cutting order above. Sew strips together ¹/₄" from the long raw edges. Press the seams toward the dark strip in each unit.

Color Family #2
Make 2 strip-pieced units.

5. Using a 60° equilateral triangle ruler, cut triangles from the strip-pieced units, alternating the direction of the point. You will have dark triangles with dark bases and light triangles with light bases. From each of the 7 strip-pieced units, cut as many triangles as possible. This jacket requires at least 20 dark triangles and 20 light triangles. You should be able to cut 5 to 6 triangles from each unit. Set aside partial pieces at the ends of the strips. If necessary, you can piece them together to make a whole triangle.

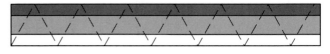

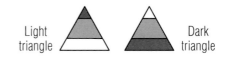

Light triangle   Dark triangle

6. Beginning at the bottom edge of the foundation back, arrange the triangles as shown below (or create your own design). To do this, position the triangles in a pleasing arrangement, row by row. Note that the triangles alternate in the rows in horizontal and vertical positions.

♪ **NOTE:** The design on the jacket back shown in the photo on page 38 was arranged and stitched in vertical rows, rather than horizontal rows as shown below.

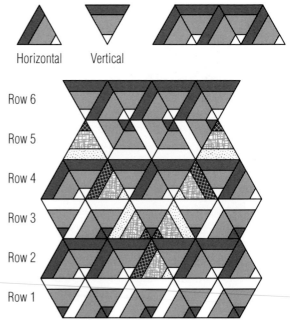

Horizontal   Vertical

Row 6
Row 5
Row 4
Row 3
Row 2
Row 1

7. When you are pleased with the design you have laid out on top of the foundation, stitch the triangles together, row by row, using $1/4$"-wide seam allowances and matching seams and raw edges. Press each seam toward one of the triangles in the pair. Then sew triangle pairs together to complete the rows. Place each completed row in position on the foundation to keep the design rows in place.

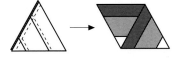

Sew triangles into pairs; sew pairs into rows.

8. To sew the rows to the foundation, begin with Row 1 at the bottom and pin it in place. Flip Row 2 down onto Row 1 with right sides together and raw edges even. Pin carefully with seam lines matching. Stitch $1/4$" from the raw edges. Turn Row 2 up onto the foundation, press, and pin in place.

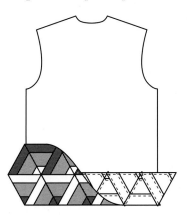

9. Sew the remaining rows to the foundation in the same manner, making sure the foundation is smooth and flat underneath. If some of the foundation shows at the top in the shoulder area after you have stitched all the triangle rows in place, add a strip of Color Family 1 Light in the same manner. Trim the patchwork even with the outer edges of the foundation and stitch $1/4$" from all raw edges. Set scraps aside.

10. Place the jacket front foundations at each side of the completed patchwork back with side seams matching. Arrange triangles of Color Family 1 and/or Family 2 in the front chest area, placing the bottom edge of the row of triangles even with the bottom edge of the triangles in Row 5 on the back. Stitch triangles together, pin in place, and trim even with the foundation. Stitch $1/4$" from the front and armhole edges.

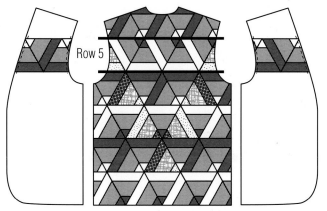

Row 5

11. *Optional:* Using perle cotton or other heavy thread, tack Tricky Triangles to the foundation at each tip of the Color Family 2 triangles in the back. Do the same to the front after other techniques are added above and below Tricky Triangles.

To tack, thread a large-eyed needle with heavy thread and double. Do not tie in a knot. Take a stitch from the right side through to the back and then back to the right side, taking a $1/4$" bite. Tie the doubled thread in a double knot on the right side of the jacket. Clip threads, leaving $1/2$"- to 1"-long tails.

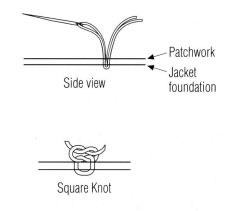

Patchwork

Jacket foundation

Side view

Square Knot

✓Boogie Bargello

MATERIALS

Color Family 1	Color Family 2
$\frac{1}{3}$ yd. Light	$\frac{1}{8}$ yd. Dark
$\frac{1}{8}$ yd. Dark	$\frac{1}{8}$ yd. Medium Dark
	$\frac{1}{16}$ yd. Medium
	$\frac{1}{8}$ yd. Medium Light
	$\frac{1}{16}$ yd. Light

DIRECTIONS

Cut all strips across the width of the fabric from selvage to selvage.

1. From Color Family 1, cut:
   1 strip of Light (A), 10" wide
   2 strips of Dark (B), each 2" wide
2. From Color Family 2, cut:
   2 strips of Dark (C), each 1$\frac{1}{2}$" wide
   2 strips of Medium Dark (D), each 2" wide
   2 strips of Medium (E), each 1" wide
   2 strips of Medium Light (F), each 1$\frac{1}{2}$" wide
   1 strip of Light (G), 2" wide
3. Arrange the strips in the order shown below and sew together, using $\frac{1}{4}$"-wide seams. Press all seams away from Strip A.

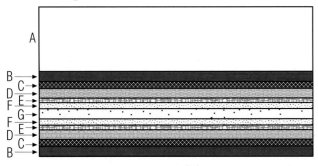

4. Fold the strip-pieced unit in half *lengthwise* with right sides together and the long raw edges of the first and last strips even. Stitch $\frac{1}{4}$" from the edge to make one long tube.

♪ **NOTE:** The strip-pieced tube should lie flat when folded in half in preparation for stitching. If it does not, stitch from the center out, only as far as it does lie flat. Cut strips from the stitched section only as directed below, cutting as many as possible before you need to realign and stitch more of the tube. Each time you cut a new series of strips, first cut a new straight edge on the tube.

5. Using a rotary cutter, ruler, and mat, cut the whole tube into rings. Cut 5 rings of *each* of the following widths: $\frac{3}{4}$"; 1"; 1$\frac{1}{4}$"; 1$\frac{1}{2}$"; 1$\frac{3}{4}$"; 2".

   After cutting the total of 30 rings, cut the remaining tube (if any) into 2"-wide rings.

$\frac{3}{4}$"	1"	1$\frac{1}{4}$".	1$\frac{1}{2}$"	1$\frac{3}{4}$"	2"

♪ **NOTE:** It is not necessary to keep the strips in any particular order as you will position them randomly to create the Bargello patchwork.

6. Cut interruption strips from Fabric B (Color Family 1 Dark) to place between the pieced Bargello strips so the finished piece will fit across the jacket fronts. Cut 1 strip of each of the following widths: 1"; 1$\frac{1}{4}$"; 1$\frac{1}{2}$". Cut additional strips later if needed.
7. To make the Bargello patchwork, you will need to open each ring you cut (step 5, above) into a strip. Where you open each ring will depend on how the design develops. You may use a scissors to cut the rings through Fabric A (Color Family 1 Light) or you may remove the stitching in a seam to open the ring at the desired location. *Do not cut the rings apart in any fabric other than Fabric A.*

   Your design will form a gradual stair-step arrangement with Fabric A (Light) covering large areas.

   The Bargello for the jacket shown in the photos on pages 36–37 was made in the following manner. You may open and arrange your Bargello in a different design if you prefer.

To open and arrange the strips:

a. Hold a Bargello ring so the seam allowances are facing down and undo the stitching between one A and B seam so that Fabric B is at the top of the opened ring. Place it on the lower right foundation front just under the Tricky Triangles and next to the side seam.

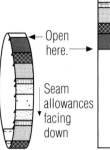

b. Select the next Bargello ring to open, choosing one of a different width than the first. Using the first Fabric E segment on the strip you placed on the foundation as a guide, cut into Fabric A in the second ring so that some of Fabric A is at the top and bottom of the strip and the Bargello begins to make a downward stair-step design. Continue doing this with each strip until Fabric B comes to the top of the Bargello design again. This should be enough to cover the right front of the jacket.

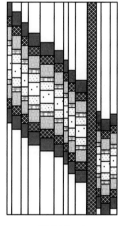

Right front

c. Sew the Bargello strips together, using ¹/₄"-wide seam allowances. For speed, stack the strips in the correct order before taking them to the sewing machine. Seams will not match from row to row. Press all seams in one direction. Periodically place the Bargello piece on the jacket foundation to determine where to add interruption strips of Fabric B. Plan their placement so that a 1¹/₂"-wide interruption strip will be 2" to 3" from the front edge of the right front. If necessary, add a strip of fabric to the side seam edge of the Bargello to cover the foundation. See illustration above right.

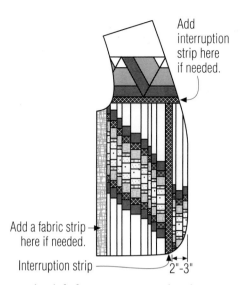

d. For the left front, continue the design even with the front edge of the right front Bargello, making the design step up with the next 4 strips, then start back down again with the fifth strip. When Fabric B ends up at the bottom of the strip and all of Fabric A is at the top, begin opening the strips between fabrics instead of cutting apart at Fabric A only. Continue opening rings and positioning strips until you have enough strips to cover the left front foundation. Sew the Bargello strips together, adding interruption strips of Fabric B as needed and where desired to cover the left front foundation. If necessary, add a strip of Fabric B to the underarm edge of the Bargello to cover the foundation.

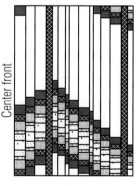

Left front

8. Place the completed Bargello pieces on the front foundations with the top edge parallel to the bottom edge of Tricky Triangles. Pin to the foundation and trim even with the foundation raw edges. Stitch ¹/₄" from the outer raw edges. If the Bargello is not long enough to cover the length of the uncovered foundation front, place a horizontal strip of Fabric B between the Tricky Triangles and the Boogie Bargello.

9. Embellish the interruption strip on the right front with buttons, beads, or charms.

✓Overlapping Flaps

MATERIALS

Color Family 1

     ¹/₄ yd. Medium Dark

     ¹/₄ yd. Medium Light

DIRECTIONS

1. From each of the fabrics, cut 4 pieces, each 7" x 8".
2. Place like fabrics *right sides together* to make 4 sets of 2 each. Layer the pairs together in 1 stack of 8 pieces.
3. With the edge of the 60° triangle parallel to the long edge of the stacked pieces, cut away the small triangle at the end as shown.

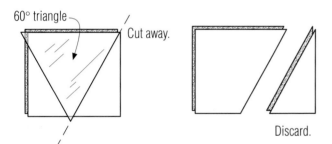

60° triangle — Cut away.

Discard.

4. Unstack into the original 4 sets of 2 each. Sew each pair together along the short edge and the angled edge you just cut. Clip the corner, turn right side out, and press. Topstitch ¹/₄" from the stitched outside edges. If desired, make a buttonhole near the corner of each of the 4 completed flaps.

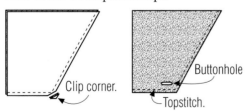

Clip corner.

Buttonhole

Topstitch.

5. Choose a fabric to cover the upper shoulder area of each foundation front. For each jacket front, cut a rectangle a little larger than necessary to cover the shoulder area. Place it on the Tricky Triangles with right sides together and raw edges even. Stitch ¹/₄" from the raw edges, then turn the fabric rectangle up onto the foundation. Pin in place, trim even with the foundation, and stitch ¹/₄" from the raw edges.

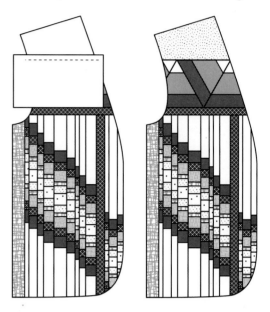

6. Place 2 completed flaps on each upper front at the shoulder, with the lower edge of the flaps even with Tricky Triangles. Position with the flap closest to the armhole on top of the other flap with a 1" triangular opening between the 2, exposing the fabric behind. Trim flaps even with the foundation edges and stitch ¹/₄" from raw edges. Sew buttons in place.

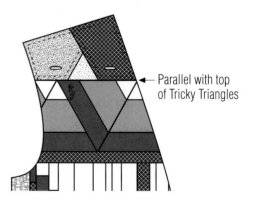

← Parallel with top of Tricky Triangles

✓Pointed Tucks

MATERIALS

Color Family 2
   $1/3$ yd. Dark
36–38 charms or buttons with shanks, about $1/4$"
   diameter, to hang from points

DIRECTIONS

Cut all strips across the width of the fabric from selvage to selvage.

1. From the dark fabric, cut 4 strips, each $2^1/2$" wide.
2. Sew 2 strips together at the short ends to make a strip approximately 84" long. Repeat with the remaining strips. You will use 1 of these for each sleeve.
3. From sturdy cardboard, cut a $1^3/8$" x 5" strip.
4. Pin 1 long strip of fabric to the wide end of the ironing board, right side up. Starting 2" from the pins, fold the fabric over the cardboard template to make a $1^3/8$"-deep tuck. There will be 2 layers of fabric on top of the cardboard strip and 1 layer under the cardboard. Press with cardboard in place, then remove cardboard and press flat again. Pin the tuck to the layer of fabric underneath.
5. Make another tuck in the same way, $1/4$" below the folded edge of the first tuck. Continue making and pressing pleats in the strip until you have a tucked strip long enough to fit the sleeve foundation. The untucked 2" section at the top of the strip will be at the top of the sleeve and there will be an untucked section approximately $1/2$" to 1" long at the bottom of the strip.

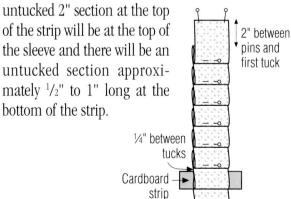

2" between pins and first tuck

$1/4$" between tucks

Cardboard strip

6. At the sewing machine, remove the pins and fold the outer raw edges of the first pleat up so the corners meet in the center. Stitch $1/16$" from the raw edges. Press flat. Continue folding and stitching the remaining tucks in the same manner.

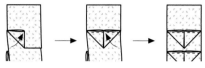

7. Beginning with the first tuck, turn the strip back on itself along the stitched edge. Stitch through all layers $3/16$" from the fold.

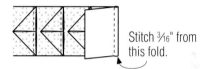

Stitch $3/16$" from this fold.

Repeat with the remaining tucks. After stitching all tucks in this manner, press flat on the triangle side of the strip. Along each long side, stitch $1/8$" from the raw edges to hold the pleats in place.

8. Tack a button or charm to the tip of each point.
9. Check the sleeve foundation to make sure it is the correct length plus $1/2$" for the seam at the bottom edge. Adjust as necessary. Check the length of the tucked strips. If they are not long enough to reach to the bottom of the sleeve, add a strip of fabric to one end of each tucked strip and make additional tucks as described above.
10. Make a lengthwise fold in each sleeve, beginning at the shoulder dot. Press to crease. Center a tucked strip over the crease line on each sleeve. Stitch to the foundation along the previous stitching.

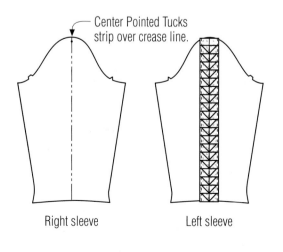

Center Pointed Tucks strip over crease line.

Right sleeve   Left sleeve

✓Square Dance

MATERIALS

Color Family 1	Color Family 2
¹/₄ yd. Medium Dark	¹/₄ yd. Medium Dark
¹/₄ yd. Medium Light	¹/₄ yd. Medium
¹/₄ yd. Light	¹/₄ yd. Medium Light

DIRECTIONS

Cut all strips across the width of the fabric from selvage to selvage.

1. From each of the fabrics listed above, cut 4 strips, each 1¹/₂" wide. You will have a total of 24 strips. Sew the strips together in the order shown below to make 4 identical strip-pieced units of 6 strips each.

| Light #1 |
| Medium Light #1 |
| Medium Dark #1 |
| Medium Dark #2 |
| Medium #2 |
| Medium Light #2 |

2. Cut 6 squares from each strip-pieced unit, using the Quilter's Rule Jr. or other 4¹/₂"-wide ruler with a 45° line. Place the 45° line along the center seam and cut along the 3 edges of the ruler. Turn and reposition the ruler so you can cut the fourth side. Save the resulting leftover triangles. Some will be A triangles (Color Family 1) and some will be B triangles (Color Family 2).

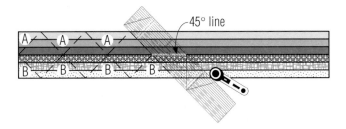

3. For each sleeve, make 2 rows of 5 to 6 squares each, arranging them to form a zigzag pattern as shown. The number needed depends on the length of the sleeve. Sew the squares together into rows and press the seams in one direction.

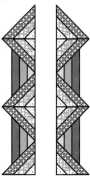

Make 4.

4. *Using a ¹/₈"-wide seam allowance,* sew sets of 2 B triangles together with 1 A triangle between each set. Add 1 B triangle to the bottom of each strip. Make an identical strip, then make 2 mirror-image strips.

Make 2 of each.

5. Sew a triangle strip to 1 long edge of each strip of squares. Press the seam to one side. Pin to the foundation on either side of the Pointed Tucks with raw edges next to each other. Trim even with foundation. Stitch ¹/₈" from the inner raw edge of the strip of squares and ¹/₄" from the outer raw edges.

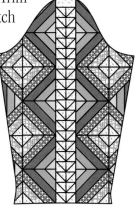

♪ **NOTE:** If desired, you may add an interruption strip (as you did with Boogie Bargello) between the strip of squares and the strip of triangles. The sleeves for the jacket shown in the photo on page 38 were made this way.

6. Cover the raw edges of the tucks and the squares with gimp or braid as shown in step 6 on page 16.

✓Tasseled Triangles

MATERIALS

2 leftover Tricky Triangles and fabric scraps to face them
Ready-made tassels or make your own using perle
cotton or other decorative yarns and threads of your
choice. See tassel directions, below.

DIRECTIONS

1. From the fabric scrap of your choice, cut a facing for each Tricky Triangle, using the triangle as a pattern.
2. Place each Tricky Triangle right sides together with its facing. Stitch ¼" from the 2 long edges. Clip across the point, turn right side out, and press. Make a buttonhole at the point.

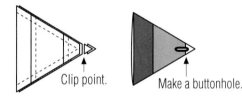

Clip point.   Make a buttonhole.

3. Place a finished triangle on each jacket front at the side seam, positioning each in a Fabric A area of Boogie Bargello. With the raw edges even, stitch the triangles to the jacket ¼" from the raw edges. Sew a button in position under the buttonhole and hand sew a tassel in place at the point.

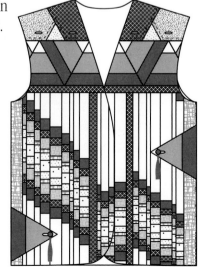

To make a tassel:

1. Cut a piece of firm cardboard the approximate desired length of the finished tassel.
2. Wind desired yarn or thread (or a combination) over the cardboard until you have the desired fullness. Slip a piece of yarn under the yarn bundle at one end of the cardboard and tie in a square knot. Cut the yarn bundle at the other end to release the tassel from the cardboard.

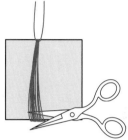

Cut yarn bundle.

3. Wrap some yarn around the tassel ½" from the tied end to form a neck. Thread yarn into a large-eyed needle and pull the needle up through the neck to the top of the tassel. Clip yarn ends close to the top of the tassel.

✓ *Jacket Finishing*

1. Apply fusible interfacing to the wrong side of the jacket fronts and the back neckline, following the manufacturer's directions. Cut 2"-wide strips of interfacing and fuse to the bottom edges of the foundation fronts, back, and sleeves.

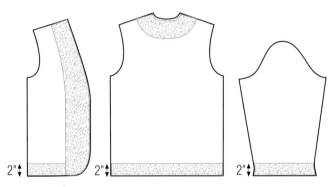

2"↕   2"↕   2"↕

Apply fusible interfacing to wrong side of jacket foundation.

2. With right sides together, stitch the jacket fronts to the back at the shoulders as shown in step 8 on page 16. Press the seam open. Repeat with the jacket lining pieces. Cover the seam line of the patchwork jacket with trim if desired.

3. Compare the completed patchwork jacket and sleeves to the lining pieces as shown in step 9 on page 17.

4. Prepare and sew the patchwork sleeves to the patchwork jacket and the lining sleeves to the lining as shown in steps 10–12 on page 17.

5. With right sides together, stitch the jacket front to the back along the underarm and sleeve seams as shown in step 13 on page 17, making sure that the underarm seams match. Repeat with the lining. Press the seams open. Complete steps 14 and 15 on page 17.

6. Beginning at the center back, pin and baste the piping to the outer edges of the jacket, positioning the piping cord ¹/₂" from the cut edge of the jacket. Overlap the ends as shown when you reach the starting point. Repeat at the bottom edge of each sleeve, starting and ending the piping close to the underarm seam. Press the seam allowance toward the foundation side of the sleeve. (No patchwork is shown in the jacket illustration above.)

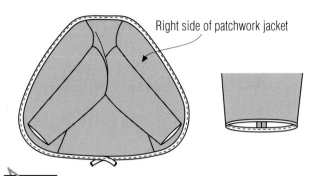

Right side of patchwork jacket

♪ **NOTE:** You may hand or machine baste. If you machine baste, use a zipper foot to stitch close to the cord as shown in step 6 on page 16.

7. Pin the lining to the outer edges of the jacket front and back with right sides together and raw edges matching. Stitch, using a zipper foot to get close to the cording. Begin and end stitching on the back, 3" from the side seams. Leave an opening for turning in the jacket back as shown.

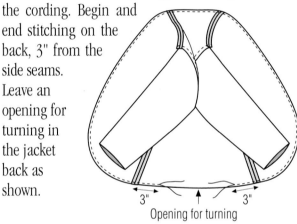

3"   3"

Opening for turning

8. Trim the seam allowance to ¹/₄", clip the neckline curves, and turn the jacket right side out through the opening at the bottom edge. Press carefully. Turn in the lining at the lower edge of the jacket back and slipstitch to the piping.

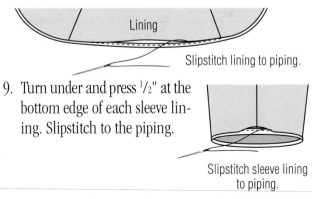

Lining

Slipstitch lining to piping.

9. Turn under and press ¹/₂" at the bottom edge of each sleeve lining. Slipstitch to the piping.

Slipstitch sleeve lining to piping.

10. Make buttonholes in the positions indicated on the pattern and sew buttons in place on the left front.

Jacket Seven by Pat Creech, Houston, Texas. Geometric shapes and florals combined give design emphasis to the high contrast of lights and darks in this striking jacket.

The placement of lights and darks in "Tricky Triangles" creates interesting secondary patterns on the jacket back.

Tuxedo Tango

- **Black Tie**
- **Wrapped Packages**
- **Christmas in a Log Cabin**
- **New Year's Streamers**
- **Ribbon Rose and Lapels**

New Year's Streamers
(page 61)

Fill-in
(step 6, page 60)

Christmas in a Log Cabin
(page 59)

Lapels with Ribbon Rose
(page 62)

Wrapped Packages
(page 58)

Fill-in
(step 13, page 56)

Black Tie
(page 55)

Fill-in
(step 14, page 57)

Fill-in
(step 8, page 59)

Jacket Eight by Barbara Weiland

PREPARATION

Cut the jacket fronts, back, and sleeves from the foundation fabric and from the lining fabric. Set the lining pieces aside.

Shopping List

All yardage requirements are based on 44"-wide fabrics, unless otherwise noted. When using the same fabric for more than one patchwork technique, combine the yardage requirements.

Jacket Foundation	2 yds. cotton flannel or muslin*
Jacket Lining	2 yds. silky lining fabric or smooth cotton fabric
Interfacing	$1/2$ yd. lightweight fusible interfacing
Shoulder Pads	Raglan-style shoulder pads ($3/8$" to $3/4$" thick)
Black Tie	$1/8$ yd. each of 4 different prints (A, B, C, and D)
	$1/8$ yd. Solid #1**
	$3/8$ yd. Solid #2 for background in Bowtie blocks and for the jacket facings
	$2^1/4$ yds. narrow trim or ribbon
Wrapped Packages	$1/4$ yd. each of Prints A, B, C, and D
	4 completed blocks left over from Black Tie (See directions on page 55.)
Christmas in a Log Cabin	Assorted ribbons and trims; amount varies depending on how much embellishment you desire (See Decorative Braid and Ribbon yardage, below.)
	Strips cut from fabric leftovers from Black Tie and Wrapped Packages (See directions.)
	1 completed block left over from Black Tie
	6" square of tear-away stabilizer
New Year's Streamers	$2/3$ yd. Solid #1 or Solid #2
	12–20 small cutaway triangles left over from Black Tie
	4" x 7" piece of paper-backed fusible web, such as Wonder-Under, or a piece of Fine Fuse and a Teflon press cloth
	8–10 yds. narrow trim, such as Radiance, for couching
Lapels	$2/3$ yd. Solid #2 (for lapel facings)
	$2/3$ yd. Solid #3 (for lapels)
	Approximately $1^1/2$ yds. rope braid or other flexible braid trim for lapel
Ribbon Rose	$1/2$ yd. of $1^1/2$"-wide wire-edged ribbon for flower
	$1/8$ yd. of $1^1/2$"-wide wire-edged ribbon for leaves

(continued)

FABRIC SELECTION TIPS

- Choose four prints and three solids for a total of seven fabrics. Make sure there is variety in the print scale, from tiny to large prints. Solids #1 and #2 will be used in the patchwork, and #3 is for the lapels. If you prefer, substitute a fifth print for Solid #1 on the jacket back.

- If you plan to use tissue lamé, metallics, or other fabrics that ravel, apply a lightweight fusible interfacing to the wrong side before cutting any of the pieces. To avoid melting or puckering delicate fabrics, choose a cool-fuse interfacing. Ask for these at your favorite fabric store. Be sure to follow the manufacturer's directions.

- The yardage given for ribbons and trims are suggestions. Buy a variety of ribbons and trims in 1- to 3-yard cuts so that you have plenty to use as you embellish the patchwork.

- Before you begin, make a fabric swatch card to identify each of your fabrics. Cut a small swatch of each fabric and label it appropriately (A, B, C, D for the prints and #1, #2, #3 for the solids).

Shopping List (continued)

Decorative Braid and Ribbon	2½ yds. for shoulder and armhole seams and bottom edge of sleeves
	3 yds. each of 2 types of narrow braid for Black Tie and Packages
	1 yd. each of 3 additional braids for Wrapped Packages
	2 yds. each of 2 types of ribbon for Wrapped Packages and Christmas in a Log Cabin
Notions	⅝ yd. 1"-wide elastic
	1 button, 1" diameter, for front closure
	5 or 6 buttons, ½" diameter, for lapel trim
	Threads to match fabrics and trims

* *Preshrink the foundation fabric, allow to dry, and press to remove wrinkles.*
** *If you wish, you may substitute a print for Solid #1 as was done in the sample jacket in the photo on page 52.*

In addition to the fabrics and notions listed, you will need the following special supplies:

Rotary cutter, mat, and 4½"-wide ruler
Removable marking pencil or tailor's chalk
Zigzag sewing machine in good working condition
Braiding foot and/or Tricot foot for your sewing machine

✓Black Tie

MATERIALS

1/8 yd. each of 4 different prints (A, B, C, and D)
1/8 yd. Solid #1*
1/3 yd. Solid #2 for background in Bowtie blocks
Approximately 2 1/4 yds. narrow trim or ribbon

If you wish, substitute a print for Solid #1 as was done in the sample jacket in the photo on page 52.

DIRECTIONS

Cut all strips across the width of the fabric from selvage to selvage.

1. From each of the 4 prints and Solid #1, cut 1 strip, 2 1/2" wide. Cut 12 squares, each 2 1/2" x 2 1/2", from each strip. From each of the same fabrics, cut 1 strip 1 1/2" wide. Cut 12 squares, each 1 1/2" x 1 1/2", from each strip.

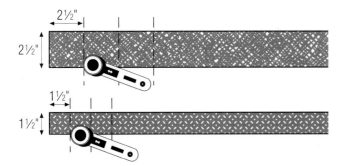

2. From Solid #2 for the block backgrounds, cut 4 strips, each 2 1/2" wide. Cut a total of 60 squares, each 2 1/2" x 2 1/2", from the strips.

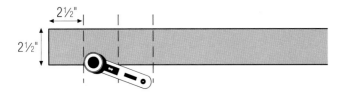

NOTE: For each Black Tie block, you will use two 2 1/2" background squares (Solid #2). You will also use two 2 1/2" squares and two 1 1/2" squares of the same fabric (one of the prints or Solid #1).

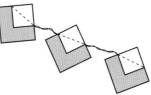

Directions follow for making one complete block. After you have made one block and understand the process, make the remaining 29 blocks, using chain piecing (page 23) to make quick work of them.

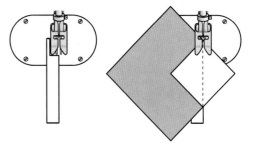

3. Place a 1 1/2" square in one corner of a background square with right sides together and raw edges even. Stitch diagonally from corner to corner.

 Stitch.

NOTE: To sew a straight line without marking each square, use this handy tip I learned from quiltmaker and author Sally Schneider. Place a piece of masking tape on your machine with the right-hand edge in front of and in line with the needle. Begin stitching exactly in the corner of the top square and keep the opposite corner pointed at the edge of the masking tape.

4. Cut away the corner $^1/_4$" from the stitching. Set cutaways aside for New Year's Streamers, page 61.

5. Press the seam toward the small triangle.

6. Repeat steps 3 and 4 to make a second square of the same fabrics.

7. With right sides together, stitch each pieced square to a 2$^1/_2$" square of matching print fabric. Press the seam toward the print square. Then stitch 2 matching units together as shown to complete 1 Black Tie block. Press.

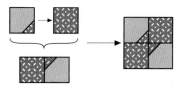

8. Repeat steps 2–7 to make the remaining 29 blocks.

9. Arrange 25 of the completed blocks, following the diagram below for fabric placement. Stitch together in 5 rows of 5 blocks each, pressing the seams in opposite directions from row to row. Sew the rows together. Set the remaining blocks aside for Wrapped Packages and Christmas in a Log Cabin.

Row 5	C	B	1	D	A
Row 4	B	1	D	A	B
Row 3	1	D	A	B	C
Row 2	D	A	B	C	D
Row 1	A	B	C	D	1

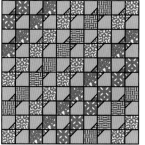

10. Draw a line on the back foundation piece $^1/_4$" below the notches from side to side and parallel to the bottom edge. Mark the center back at the neckline edge and on the line you drew at the bottom.

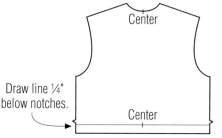

11. Position the completed patchwork piece on the back foundation with the bottom edge even with the drawn line and the center of the completed patchwork matching the center back lines on the foundation. Pin in place. Turn over and trim patchwork even with foundation around the neckline, shoulders, and armholes. Stitch the patchwork to the foundation $^1/_4$" from the raw edges of the neckline and armholes.

♪ **NOTE:** The patchwork will not cover the foundation entirely at the side seams.

12. Add trim to the 4 vertical seams in the patchwork. To attach the trim, use a zigzag or straight stitch, using a braiding, piping, or tricot foot, if available for your machine, to make trim application easier.

13. Add a strip of background fabric to each side of the patchwork to fill in the underarm area as needed. Cut a strip slightly wider than the area to be covered and position on top of the patchwork with right sides together and raw edges even. Stitch through all layers, then press toward the foundation, pin in place, trim even with edges of foundation, and stitch $^1/_4$" from the raw edges.

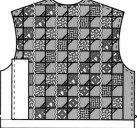

Stitch background strip to patchwork and foundation.

♪ **NOTE:** If there are areas at the shoulder seams that are not covered by the patchwork, add background fabrics as described above to cover the foundation.

14. Cut a 2"-wide strip of the background fabric or a print and pin to the bottom edge of the patchwork with right sides together and raw edges even. Stitch $1/4$" from the raw edges through all layers. Press the strip toward the foundation and trim even with the bottom edge. This is the hem allowance and will not show in the finished jacket.

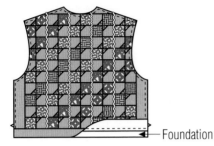

— Foundation

15. Turn under $1/4$" at the lower edge of the jacket back and press. Edgestitch (topstitch very close to the finished edge.)

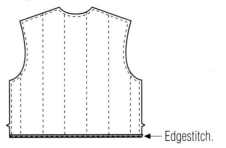

— Edgestitch.

16. Set completed jacket back aside.

✓ *Wrapped Packages*

MATERIALS

¹/₄ yd. each of Prints A, B, C, and D
4 completed blocks left over from Black Tie (2 of the
  block with Solid #1 and 2 of the block with Print C)
8–9 yds. narrow trim or ribbon

DIRECTIONS

Cut all strips across the width of the fabric from selvage to selvage.

1. From each of the 4 prints, cut 2 strips, each 4¹/₂"
   wide. Sew strips together in alphabetical order to
   make 2 strip-pieced units, each approximately
   16¹/₂" x 42". Crosscut each unit into segments 4¹/₂"
   wide. You will need 18 segments.

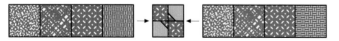

Make 2 strip-pieced units.
Cut a total of 18 segments.

2. Sew a segment to each side of each of the 4 Black Tie
   blocks as shown, paying careful attention to the
   placement of the tie in the strip.

3. Fold each sleeve in half lengthwise and press a crease.
   Open out each sleeve and place on a flat surface,
   making sure that the right side of each sleeve is
   facing up so you have a left and a right sleeve. Draw
   a line ¹/₄" below the hem fold line and parallel to the
   bottom edge, on each sleeve foundation.

4. Working on 1 sleeve foundation at a time, place a
   strip with the point of the Black Tie block on the
   crease line. Arrange so that the strip extends to the

line you drew below the hem line. Pin in place. Trim
excess strip and set aside.

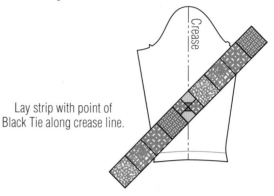

Lay strip with point of
Black Tie along crease line.

5. Pin a second pieced strip to the top edge of the first
   strip with right sides together and raw edges even,
   making sure that when stitched and flipped onto the
   foundation, the second Black Tie block will lie di-
   rectly above the first. Pin carefully so that seam lines
   match. Stitch ¹/₄" from the raw edges. Press strip
   toward foundation. Repeat steps 4 and 5 on the remaining sleeve foundation.

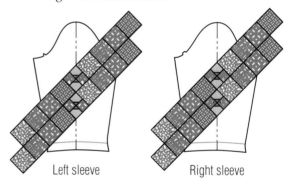

Left sleeve   Right sleeve

♪ **NOTE:** If you want the sleeves to be mirror im-
ages of each other, place the pieced strips on the
diagonal in the opposite direction from those on
the first sleeve.

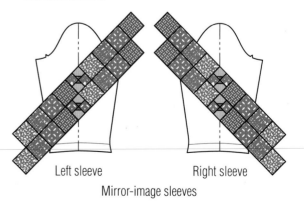

Left sleeve   Right sleeve

Mirror-image sleeves

6. Using the remaining pieced segments and the same method of stitching and pressing, cover the foundation with patchwork. Sew segments together when necessary to make them long enough to cover the foundation. Set leftovers aside.

7. Cover seams with assorted ribbon and trims (or use all one trim as shown in the jacket in the photo on page 52) and zigzag or straight-stitch in place.

8. Stitch a strip of background fabric to the bottom of each sleeve to cover the foundation hem allowance, placing the top edge ½" (or more if a wider "cuff" is desired) above the hem fold line as shown. Cover the raw edge with decorative braid or trim and zigzag in place. Stitch ¼" from the outer edges of each sleeve. Set completed sleeves aside.

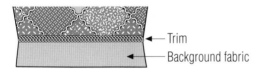
← Trim
← Background fabric

✓Christmas in a Log Cabin

MATERIALS

Assorted ribbons and trims; amount required varies depending on how much embellishment you desire
Strips cut from Black Tie and Wrapped Packages fabric leftovers (See step 7 on page 60.)
1 completed block left over from Black Tie (Print A)
6" square of tear-away stabilizer

DIRECTIONS

1. Place the right front foundation right side up on a flat surface. Place the lapel pattern on the foundation and trace the outside edge onto the foundation. You will cover the entire foundation with fabric strips and ribbon and trim, but keep in mind the area that will be covered by the lapel and don't put bulky trims in that area.

2. Position the remaining Black Tie block on the foundation on point, placing it equidistant from the front and bottom edges. Pin in place, then zigzag around outer edges through all layers.

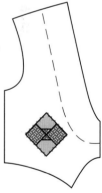

3. Turn the foundation over and position the square of stabilizer over the area where the block was stitched. Baste in place. You will add pieces around the block and sew on the bias grain of the fabric, and the stabilizer will prevent stretching while you stitch.

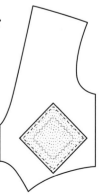

Baste tear-away stabilizer in place.

4. Using the Log Cabin piecing method, add ribbons, trims, and fabric strips around the Black Tie block to cover the foundation. Beginning at the lower right edge of the block, place the first ribbon on top of the block ¼" in from the edge and edgestitch in place. Be sure to leave at least ⅜" extra ribbon extending beyond the edge of the block at each end. Trim excess after adding the next piece of ribbon.

5. Add a piece of the same ribbon to the lower left side of the block. Switch to a different ribbon and add to the upper left and then to the upper right block edges.

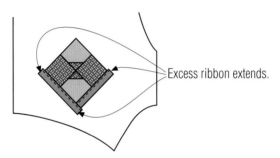

Excess ribbon extends.

6. Continue adding ribbons or trims in the same manner in a clockwise direction until you can no longer add matching strips to the right and left bottom edges of the Black Tie block. Cover the exposed foundation below the trims with one of the fabrics. Tuck the fabric raw edge under the outer edge of the ribbon or trim before stitching in place.

Tuck fabric under unstitched
edge of ribbon; then stitch.

Fill in these areas
with fabric.

NOTE: If you prefer, you can use 1½"-wide fabric strips in place of ribbons around the Bow Tie block. Place strips face down with raw edges even with the block. Stitch ¼" from the raw edge, then turn onto the foundation and press before adding the next fabric strip.

7. Cover the foundation above the block with a single fabric or with strips cut from Bow Tie and Wrapped Packages fabric leftovers as shown in the jacket on page 52. Cut strips of varying widths from the print and/or solid fabrics and sew to the foundation in the same manner as you added pieced segments to the sleeves.

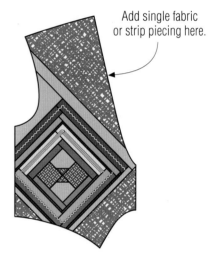

Add single fabric
or strip piecing here.

8. Turn the right front over and carefully tear away the stabilizer. Use a tweezers to remove small bits that remain under the stitching.

9. Add ribbons and trims as desired to embellish the completed patchwork.

10. Stitch ¼" from the raw edges of the foundation.

✓New Year's Streamers

MATERIALS

²/₃ yd. Solid #1 or Solid #2 for left front

12–20 small cutaway triangles left over from Black Tie

4" x 7" piece of paper-backed fusible web, such as Wonder-Under, or a piece of Fine Fuse and a Teflon press cloth

8–10 yds. narrow trim, such as Radiance or other specialty thread or yarn, for couching

DIRECTIONS

1. Cut a left vest front from the solid fabric for background. Pin to the right side of the left front foundation. Stitch ¹/₄" from all raw edges.

2. Place the lapel pattern on top of the left front in position and lightly mark its outer edge on the background fabric. Place all triangles (step 3, below) outside this marked line.

Mark edge of lapel on background fabric.   Left front

3. Select 12–20 cutaway triangles from the Black Tie blocks. Place the paper-backed fusible web on the ironing board with the web facing up. Place the cutaway triangles wrong side down on the fusible web and place a Teflon press cloth on top. Fuse for 2 seconds, or until the fusible web is just adhered to the triangles. Allow to cool, then cut out the triangles.

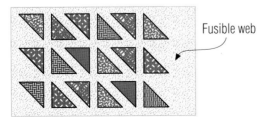

Fusible web

4. Arrange the triangles on the left front (but not in the area that will be covered by the lapel). Position so that the edges of the triangles follow common lines as much as possible. Using a removable marking pencil or tailor's chalk, draw couching lines along triangle edges onto the background fabric. These lines will be covered by couching thread, yarn, or trim.

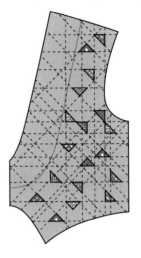

5. Remove the paper backing on each triangle and fuse in position on the left front.

6. Place couching trim on a line along a row of triangles, beginning at one raw edge of front. Zigzag over trim, being sure to catch the edge of the triangles in the stitching. When completed, all edges of each triangle should be covered by couching. Use a tricot or beading foot on your machine if available. It will help guide the trim, leaving both hands free to guide the fabric as you stitch.

✓Ribbon Rose and Lapels

MATERIALS

²/₃ yd. Solid #2
²/₃ yd. Solid #3
1¹/₂ yds. rope braid or other flexible braid trim for lapel
¹/₂ yd. of 1¹/₂"-wide wire-edged ribbon for flower
¹/₈ yd. of 1¹/₂"-wide wire-edged ribbon for leaves
5 or 6 buttons, ¹/₂" diameter, for embellishment

DIRECTIONS

1. Using the lapel pattern, cut 2 lapels from Solid #3 and 2 lapel facings from Solid #2. Cut 2 lapels from lightweight fusible interfacing. Apply interfacing to the wrong side of the lapels, following manufacturer's directions and making sure that you have a left and right lapel.

2. Arrange rope braid trim on each lapel in an undulating pattern and stitch in place. You may make the design a mirror-image or different on each lapel.

3. With right sides together, stitch each lapel to a lapel facing along the curved outer edge. Trim seam to ¹/₄", turn, and press. Set lapels aside.

4. Fold the ¹/₂ yd. length of wire-edged ribbon in half crosswise and hold raw edges with one hand. With

the other hand, pull the 2 wires on the bottom edge to gather the ribbon. Unfold the ribbon.

5. Fold one raw edge down to meet the bottom edge of ribbon, forming a 45° angle.

6. Begin wrapping the ribbon around itself at the folded end. As you do so, move gathers slightly away from the center in order to create a tight center in the rose.

7. Continue wrapping, incorporating more and more gathers and using matching thread to whipstitch the bottom edges together as you shape the ribbon into a rose. When you reach the end, turn under the remaining raw edge at a 45° angle and stitch in place.

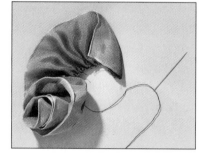

8. To make the leaves, cut the ¹/₈-yard length of ribbon into 2 equal lengths. Fold the raw edges of each as shown. Pinch and stitch to the back of the rose.

9. Use wire edges to shape the rose as desired. For a realistic look, primp the rose by turning some of the wire edges down and leaving others up. Set the completed rose aside. Attach it after completing the jacket.

✓ Jacket Finishing

1. With raw edges even, baste a finished lapel to each jacket front along the shoulder and front edges.

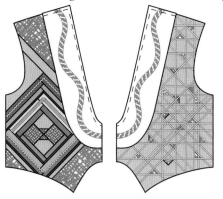

Baste lapels to front and shoulder edges.

2. With right sides together, stitch the jacket fronts to the back at the shoulders as shown in step 8 on page 16. Press the seams open. Center trim over each shoulder seam and stitch in place.

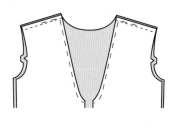

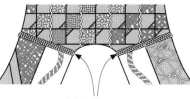

Add trim over shoulder seams.

3. Stitch the lining fronts to the back at the shoulders and press the seams open.

4. Compare the completed patchwork jacket and sleeves to the lining pieces as shown in step 9 on page 17 .

5. Trim away 1¼" at the lower edge of the lining back and from the bottom edge of each lining sleeve.

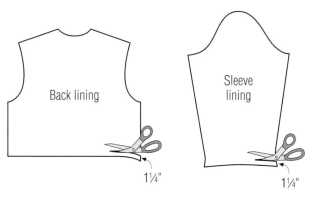

6. Prepare and sew the patchwork and lining sleeves to the jacket and the lining as shown in steps 10–12 on page 17.

7. Fuse interfacing to the wrong side of the front and back neck facings. Stitch the front facings to the back facing at the shoulders. Trim the seams to ¼" and press open. Finish the inner edges of the facing with zigzag stitching or serging, or turn under ¼", press, and edgestitch.

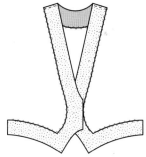

8. With right sides together, stitch the lining front to the back, matching underarm seams. Press seams open.

9. With right sides together, stitch the jacket side seams. End stitching ½" from the bottom edge of the jacket front. The bottom edge of the jacket back should extend 1" below the bottom edge of the jacket front.

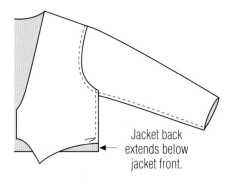

Jacket back extends below jacket front.

10. Complete step 14 on page 17. Sew shoulder pads in place as shown in step 15 on page 17.

11. Place the lining and jacket wrong sides together with raw edges even. Stitch ¼" from raw edges.

12. With right sides together, stitch the facing to the jacket along the back neckline, front neckline, and bottom edges. Trim the seam to ¼", clip curves and corners, and turn the facing to the inside. Press.

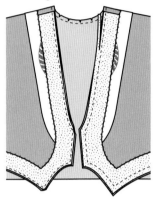

13. Understitch the remaining seam allowance to the facing around the neckline, front, and bottom edges. You will need to start and stop at the corners and you will not be able to stitch all the way into them.

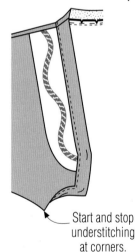

Start and stop understitching at corners.

14. Turn up the hem at the bottom edge of the jacket back. Hand sew in place, leaving unstitched at the side seams to create a casing for elastic.

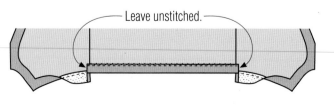

Leave unstitched.

15. Cut a piece of elastic the correct length for your size.

Extra Small: 13⅜"	Large: 18⅜"
Small: 15"	Extra Large: 20"
Medium: 16⅞"	

16. Insert the elastic into the casing. Pin securely in place at each end. Adjust the fit if necessary and cut away any excess elastic. From the right side of the jacket, stitch in-the-ditch of the side seams to hold the elastic in place.

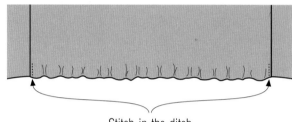

Stitch-in-the-ditch
to secure elastic ends.

17. Turn the front facing up and slipstitch in place.

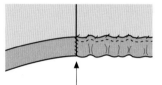

Slipstitch front facing in place.

18. Hem the jacket sleeves over the lining.

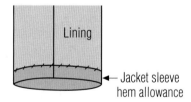

Lining

Jacket sleeve
hem allowance

19. Make a buttonhole in the right jacket front at the location marked on the pattern for Jacket 8. Sew button in position on the left front to match button-hole location.

20. Embellish the right lapel with buttons and sew the Ribbon Rose in place on the left lapel.

*Jacket Eight by Pat Creech, Houston, Texas.
Careful placement of the design elements
and trims emphasizes the vest-front styling
in Pat's jacket.*

*Pat eliminated the back elastic (page 64)
for a less fitted look in her finished jacket.*

Fandango Weave

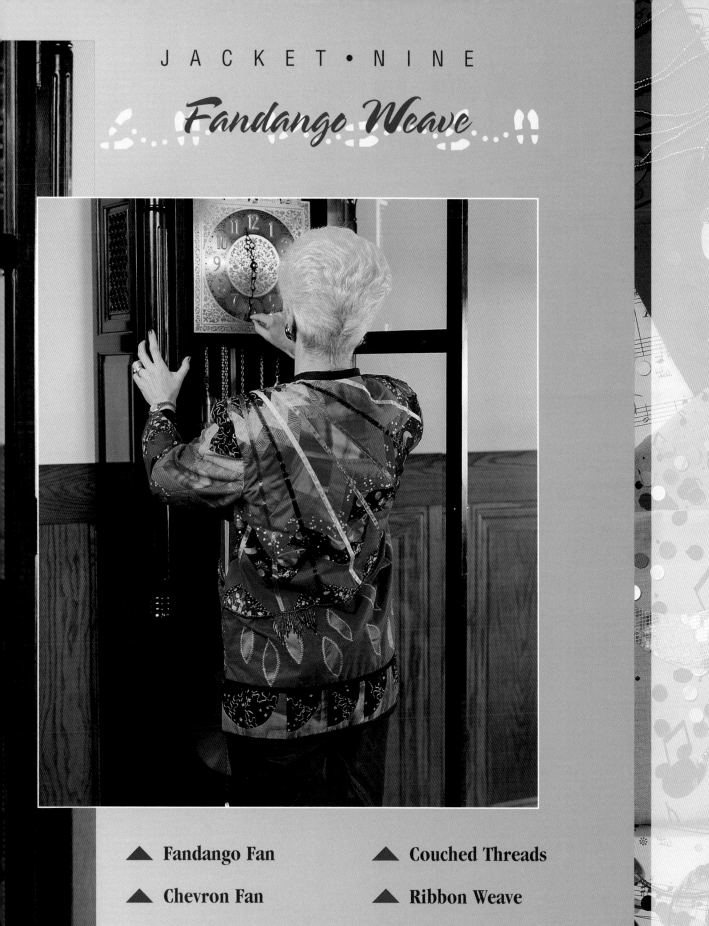

- ▲ Fandango Fan
- ▲ Chevron Fan
- ▲ Drunkard's Path
- ▲ Teardrops
- ▲ Couched Threads
- ▲ Ribbon Weave
- ▲ Tucked Medley
- ▲ Crossroads

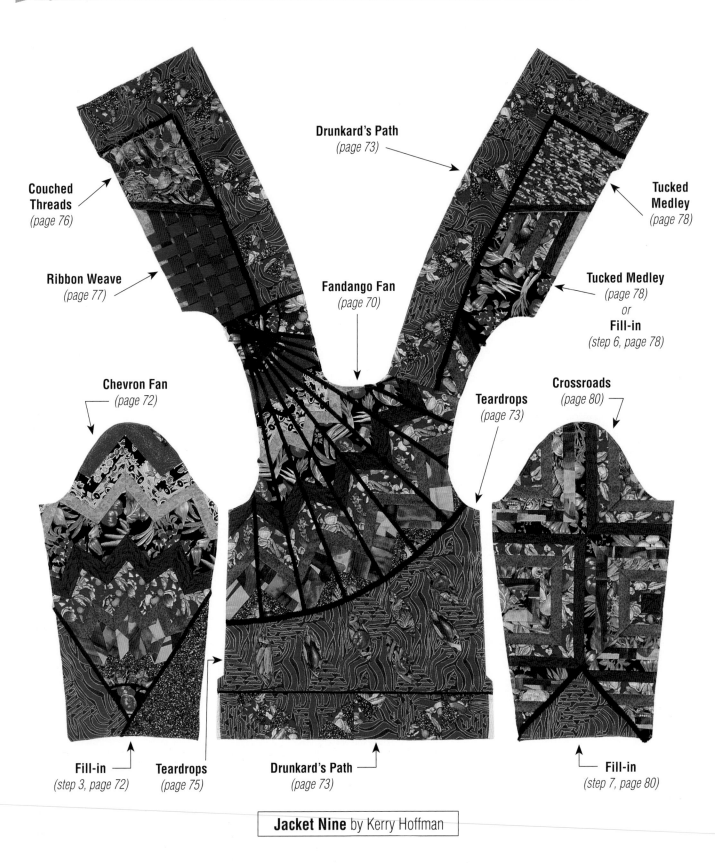

Couched Threads
(page 76)

Ribbon Weave
(page 77)

Chevron Fan
(page 72)

Drunkard's Path
(page 73)

Fandango Fan
(page 70)

Tucked Medley
(page 78)

Tucked Medley
(page 78)
or
Fill-in
(step 6, page 78)

Teardrops
(page 73)

Crossroads
(page 80)

Fill-in
(step 3, page 72)

Teardrops
(page 75)

Drunkard's Path
(page 73)

Fill-in
(step 7, page 80)

Jacket Nine by Kerry Hoffman

Shopping List

All yardage requirements are based on 44"-wide fabrics, unless otherwise noted. When using the same fabric for more than one patchwork technique, combine the yardage requirements.

Jacket Foundation	2–2³/₄ yds. cotton flannel or muslin*
Jacket Lining	2–2³/₄ yds. silky lining fabric or smooth cotton fabric
Interfacing	¹/₂ yd. lightweight fusible interfacing
Shoulder pads	Raglan-style shoulder pads (³/₈" to ³/₄" thick)
Fandango Fan and Chevron Fan	12 different fabrics (See "Fabric Selection Tips," at right.)
Drunkard's Path	¹/₄ yd. each of Fabrics #1, #2, and #6
Teardrops	¹/₃ yd. of Fabric #3
	Leftovers of Fabric #1
	10" x 18" piece of FineFuse and a Teflon press cloth
Couched Threads	¹/₃ yd. each of Fabrics #3 and #4
Ribbon Weave	9" square of synthetic suede, such as UltraSuede® brand fabric
Crossroads	3"-wide strip each of Fabrics #1, #2, #3, #5, #7, and #8
Tucked Medley	¹/₄ yd. each of Fabrics #4, #5, #7, and #9
Braid	3 yds. for covering seams
Piping	3 yds. for seams
Ribbons	2 yds. each of 4 colors, approximately ¹/₄" wide
Notions	1 large button to embellish Fandango Fan
	¹/₃ yd. dangling bead trim**
	1 package loose beads
	3 yds. of prestrung beads for embellishment
	Threads to match fabric and trims
	Metallic thread for appliqué
	Cloisonné, Radiance, or other special fibers for couching

* Preshrink the foundation fabric, allow to dry, and press to remove wrinkles.
** If dangling beads are not available in your area, write to Sew What Bernina, 4310 Dowlen Road #2, Beaumont, Texas 77706.

In addition to the fabrics and notions listed, you will need the following special supplies:
> Braiding, piping, or tricot foot
> 4" Drunkard's Path templates (#QR-401 from Quilter's Rule, Inc.). You can make your own templates, using the patterns on page 74. (The stores listed in the acknowledgments carry this tool and would be happy to send it to you by mail. Call them for ordering information.)
> Rotary cutter with small blade
> Perfect Pleater or EZE PLEATER
> 9° Circle Wedge Ruler by Marilyn Doheny (Omnigrid)
> 45° x 90° triangle ruler (45° Diamond by Quilter's Rule, Inc.)

FABRIC SELECTION TIPS

- Choose a total of twelve fabrics. Make sure there is variety in the print scale, from small to large. Include geometrics, stripes, solids, and figurative prints.
- Plan to use your two most favorite fabrics as Fabrics #1 and #2 and purchase a total of ²/₃ yard of each.
- You will need ¹/₂ yard of each of your next three favorites for Fabrics #3, #4, and #5.
- Purchase ¹/₄ yard each of Fabrics #6, #7, #8, and #9.
- You will need ¹/₈ yard of Fabrics #10, #11, and #12.
- Before you begin the patchwork, make a fabric swatch card to identify each of your fabrics by number to avoid confusion.

PREPARATION

1. Cut the jacket back, fronts, and sleeves from the foundation fabric and from the lining. Set the lining pieces aside.
2. Cut 2 front interfacings from lightweight fusible interfacing and fuse one to the wrong side of each jacket front. Cut the back neck facing from fusible interfacing and fuse to the wrong side of the jacket back.
3. Sew the left front jacket foundation to the jacket back foundation at the shoulder. Press the seam open. Set the other foundation pieces aside.

✓*Fandango Fan*

MATERIALS

Strips cut from Fabrics #1–#12 (step 1, below)

DIRECTIONS

Cut all strips across the width of the fabric from selvage to selvage.

1. Following the chart below, cut 2 strips of each fabric in the width indicated.

Fabric	Strip Width
#1, #6	3"
#2	1"
#3, #8	2½"
#4, #5, #10, #11	2"
#7, #9, #12	1½"

2. Lay out the strips in 2 identical sets, arranging the strips as desired to create color/value contrast. Use a strip that is an accent color for the center. It is not necessary to keep the strips in numerical order.

3. Sew the strips together to make 2 staggered opposing sets. Stagger 1 set to the left and 1 set to the right; stitch. (See illustration above right.) To stagger the strips, fold the short end of each strip down to meet the long edge (45° angle) as shown and crease. Open out the corner and place the short end of the next strip at the crease as shown. Continue staggering in this manner for the first strip set, then stagger from the opposite end for the second strip set. Press the seams up in one set and down in the other set.

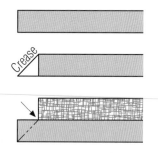

4. Cut as many wedges as possible from each set, using the Circle Wedge ruler as shown. Alternate the ruler position with each cut, making opposite angle cuts. To do this, position the 45° line on the Circle Wedge ruler parallel to a seam line on the stitched sets. *Use the same seam line to position the ruler for each new cut.*

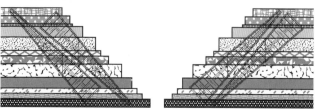

5. Stack like wedges together. You will have 4 stacks of 4 to 5 wedges each. Of the 4 stacks, 2 will have 1 color at the wide end, and the other 2 will have another color at the wide end.

6. Arrange the wedges into 2 Chevron fans, placing the wide and narrow ends of mirror-image pairs together. You will create 2 different Chevron fans, one for the Fandango Fan for the upper left back and front shoulder, the other for the Chevron fan on the left sleeve. Sew the pieces for each fan together, using ¼"-wide seams. Press seams in one direction.

♪ **NOTE:** If one fan has fewer wedges than the other, save it for the left sleeve, using the larger fan for the jacket back.

7. Place the left front/back foundation right side up on a flat surface. Place the large end of the Fandango Fan on the foundation back with the narrow end coming across the left shoulder onto the left front. Pin in place, then trim fan even with edges of foundation. Add a piece of fabric of your choice to fill in

the area to the left of the fan on the jacket front. Stitch ¹/₄" from the outer cut edges. *Do not stitch the bottom edge of the fan to the jacket back yet.*

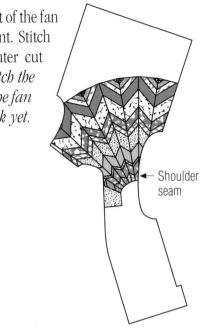

Shoulder seam

10. Position the piped edge of the quarter-circle over the raw edges of the fan and stitch in place, using your braiding or piping foot.

NOTE: You will add ribbon embellishment after you have added patchwork to the remainder of the left front.

8. Cut a quarter circle of Fabric #2 or other contrasting fabric of your choice to fill in the space just below the fan on the left front shoulder and create a straight line at the lower edge that is perpendicular to the armhole seam. Use the template on this page, adjusting as necessary to fit your jacket front.

9. With right sides together, stitch piping (as shown in step 6 on page 16) to the curved edge of the fabric quarter-circle. Press the seam toward the quarter-circle.

Pipe the curved edge.

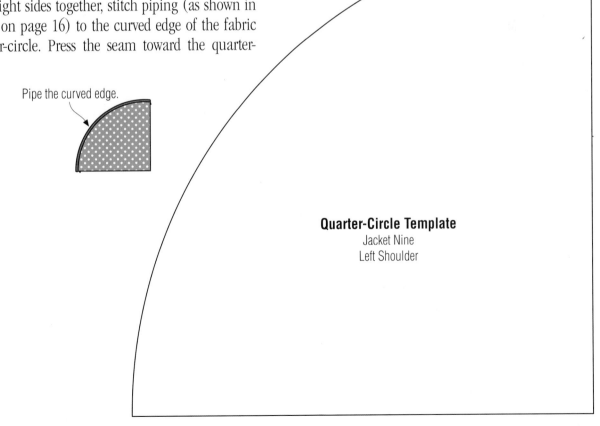

Quarter-Circle Template
Jacket Nine
Left Shoulder

✓ Chevron Fan

MATERIALS

Chevron Fan (made at the same time you made
Fandango Fan)
Fabric #2 or other contrasting fabric

DIRECTIONS

1. Identify the left and right sleeve foundations. Fold
each in half lengthwise at the shoulder dot and press
to create a crease. Set the right sleeve aside. Place the
left sleeve right side up on a flat surface.

Shoulder

Left sleeve

2. Locate and mark the center of the Chevron Fan.
Position the fan on the sleeve with centers matching
and the wide end of the fan at the top of the sleeve.
Pin in place, then trim even with the edges of the
sleeve foundation.

    If the sleeve foundation shows at the bottom
edge of the fan, add a fabric quarter-circle piece to
the bottom edge of the fan. Use the Drunkard's
Path template on page 74 to cut the quarter-circle.

Finish the curved edge with piping as you did for the
quarter-circle on the left front fan. See step 9 in
Fandango Fan on page 71.

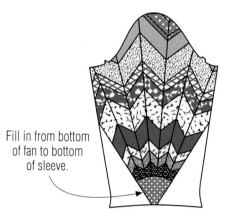

Fill in from bottom
of fan to bottom
of sleeve.

3. Cover the remaining foundation to the right and left
of the fan with Fabric #2 or other contrasting fabric.
Place fabric right sides together with outer fan edge
and stitch through all layers, using a 1/4"-wide seam
allowance. Turn the fabric toward the foundation,
pin in place, and trim edges even with the foundation. Stitch 1/4" from the raw edges.

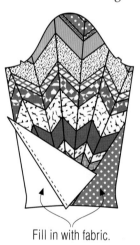

Fill in with fabric.

4. *Optional:* Embellish the seams on each side of the
fan with decorative machine stitching, couch a decorative thread in place over the seam, or cover the
seam with braid, ribbon, or trim as desired.

✓*Drunkard's Path*

MATERIALS

¹/₄ yd. each of Fabrics #1, #2, and #6

DIRECTIONS

Cut all strips across the width of the fabric from selvage to selvage.

1. From Fabric #1, cut 3 background strips, each 4¹/₂" wide. Set aside for step 9, below.
2. For the fan wedges, cut 2 strips, each 2³/₄" wide, from each of Fabrics #2 and #6. Open out all cut strips and layer in the following sequence with *right sides facing up:* #2/#6/#2/#6.
3. Crosscut the stacked strips into 2³/₄" x 4¹/₄" rectangles.

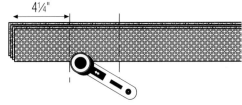

4. Cut the rectangles diagonally from the upper right corner to the lower left corner. *Be sure to make all cuts in this direction.*

Cut each stack of rectangles in the same direction.

5. Make 1 stack of all the resulting triangle stacks with all triangles facing right side up.
6. Keep this chant in mind as you follow this step: Move it over. Flip it over.
   a. Remove the first triangle from the stack and move it to the right.
   b. Remove next triangle and place it between the first triangle and the stack.

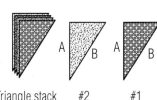

Triangle stack   #2   #1

   c. Flip triangle #1 over onto the right side of triangle #2, aligning side A of #1 with side B of #2. Stitch ¹/₄" from the raw edge.

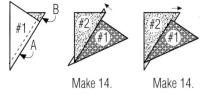

Make 14.   Make 14.

Make a total of 28 sets of triangles in this manner. In one set of 14, finger-press the seams toward the left-hand triangle in each pair. In the remaining set, finger-press the seam toward the right-hand triangle. Chain-sew to make quick work of this step.

7. Add a third triangle to 14 of the 28 sets in the same manner to create 14 wedges, each made of 3 triangles. The 2 outer triangles in each wedge should be Fabric #2 and the other one should be Fabric #6. Repeat with the remaining 14 sets. The 2 outer triangles in these wedges should be Fabric #6 and the other one should be Fabric #2. Make 14. Make 14.

8. Using the 4" Drunkard's Path templates (#QR-401 from Quilter's Rule, Inc.) or the templates on page 74, cut 28 concave units (Template B) from the 4¹/₂" background fabric strips. Save the teardrop shapes that are left over for the jacket back.

♪ **NOTE:** It is easier to cut around these curves using the rotary cutter with the smaller blade.

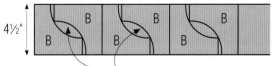

4¹/₂"

Save teardrops between pieces.

9. Cut Template A from the pieced wedge units, being careful to center the point in the center triangle in each wedge. Cut 14.   Cut 14.

10. With right sides together, pin each piece A to a piece B, matching the outer edges and the centers. Stitch ¹/₄" from the raw edges with A on the bottom. Stitch

gently and slowly, smoothing out B to avoid any puckers. Press the seam toward B. Now you should have 28 Drunkard's Path blocks. This should be enough for most jacket sizes. If necessary, make additional blocks for larger jacket sizes.

Make 14.

Make 14.

11. Beginning in one corner of the first jacket front, place a Drunkard's Path block even with the bottom and front edges of the jacket. Repeat on the other jacket front, then lay out the remaining blocks along the bottom and center front edges of the left and right fronts. Lay blocks along the bottom edge of the jacket back. Add background fabric to fill in leftover foundation at the side seams if a complete block will not fit. On the right front, the blocks go all the way to the shoulder, but on the left front, they end at the bottom edge of Fandango Fan. Position the fans as shown in the illustration at right, or as shown in the jacket on page 68.

Pin the corner block in place on the foundation, then add the next block with right sides together and raw edges even. Stitch 1/4" from the raw edges through all layers.

Continue adding blocks in this manner, but as the front edge begins to curve, take a deeper seam on the inner edge of the blocks so that they curve as needed. Sew the blocks to the bottom edge of the jacket fronts and back in the same manner. Begin with the center block on the jacket back and add blocks to the left and right of it.

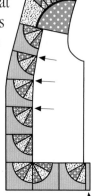

Sew deeper seams at arrows to shape blocks to fit.

Add background fabric here.

My thanks to Betty Gall of Quilter's Rule, Inc. for generously sharing this technique with me, especially for Jacket Jazz Encore.

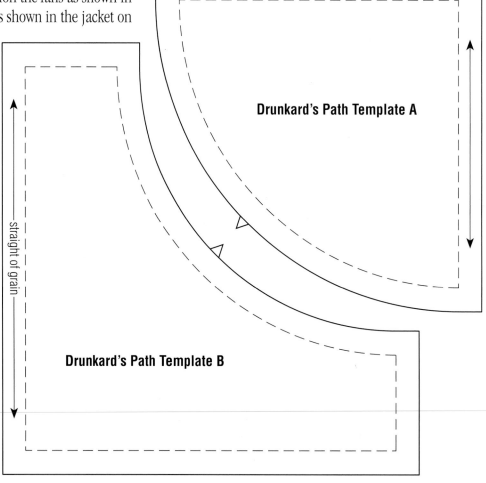

1/4" seam allowance

straight of grain

Drunkard's Path Template A

Drunkard's Path Template B

✓*Teardrops*

MATERIALS

Fabric #3 (background)
Leftovers of Fabric #1 (from Drunkard's Path, step 8, page 73)
10" x 18" piece of fusible web (Wonder-Under or Fine Fuse and a Teflon press cloth)

DIRECTIONS

1. On the jacket back, trim the points from the bottom edge of Fandango Fan to create a smooth curve.

2. Place the background fabric for Teardrops on the foundation back to cover the foundation from the bottom edge of Fandango Fan to the top edge of the Drunkard's Path border. Cut the piece large enough so that you can tuck ½" of it under the bottom edge of the trimmed Fandango Fan. Pin in place. Trim fabric even with the outer edges of the foundation and stitch ¼" from the raw edges at the side seams, *leaving the upper edge free for now.*

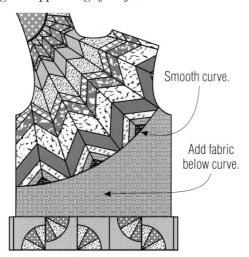

Smooth curve.

Add fabric below curve.

3. Starting at the edge on the jacket back, pin ribbon over the fan seam lines between fan blades and bring over the shoulder to the front. Anchor with pins, leaving the ends free in front. Machine or hand baste the ribbon to the bottom edge of the fan.

4. Using a piping or braiding foot and with right sides together, sew piping to the bottom edge of the fan, being careful not to catch the foundation or the background fabric in the stitching. Press the seam toward the fan and topstitch the fan edge in place on top of the background fabric. Add a row of beads next to the piping on top of the fan.

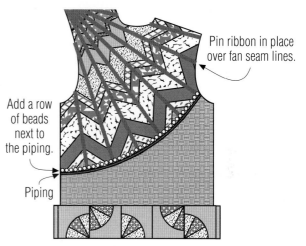

Pin ribbon in place over fan seam lines.

Add a row of beads next to the piping.

Piping

5. Select 12 teardrops from those you set aside when you made the Drunkard's Path blocks. Apply fusible web (Fine Fuse or Wonder-Under) to the *wrong side* of the teardrops, following the manufacturer's directions. Allow to cool, then remove the paper backing if using paper-backed fusible web.

Fusible web

6. Position teardrops on the jacket back in the desired arrangement below the fan and fuse in place. Using decorative thread and a satin stitch or other decorative stitch, sew each teardrop in place through all layers.

Stitch over edge of each teardrop.

 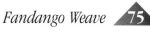

✓ Couched Threads

MATERIALS

1/3 yd. each of Fabrics #3 and #4
Decorative thread and couching thread or yarn of your
  choice

DIRECTIONS

1. Cut the jacket pocket pattern from the foundation
   fabric and from the lining fabric. Also cut the pocket
   from Fabric #3, cutting it 1/2" larger all around to
   allow for shrinkage caused by stitching.
2. Center the Fabric #3 pocket on top of the foundation
   pocket with right sides facing up. Pin.
3. Replace the regular presser foot with a couching or
   zigzag presser foot.
4. Place the couching thread in a small plastic bag and
   tape the bag to the table surface in front of your
   sewing machine. This prevents the ball of fiber from
   rolling around as you stitch.
5. Place the end of the couching yarn on the pocket
   fabric and zigzag over the yarn to hold it in place.
   The stitches do not need to penetrate the couching
   yarn. Stitch 'round and 'round, up and down, any-
   where you want to go. Just have fun stitching!

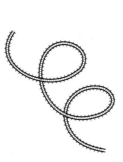

Zigzag over
yarns to couch.

6. Cut a 1 1/2"-wide band of Fabric #4 or other contrasting fabric of your choice, cutting it 2" longer than the
   length of the top edge of the couched pocket. Position
   the raw edge of the fabric strip 1" below the top edge
   of the pocket. Stitch 1/4" from the raw edge. Press the
   band toward the top of the pocket. Pin in place. Trim
   excess band even with pocket top edge and sides.

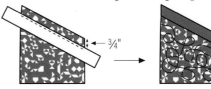

Stitch band to pocket.   Trim even with pocket.

7. With right sides together, stitch the pocket lining to
   the top edge of the couched pocket. Turn the lining to
   the wrong side of the pocket
   and press. Trim the couched
   pocket even with the lining
   edges. Stitch 1/8" from the
   raw edges.

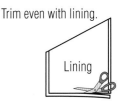

Trim even with lining.

Lining

8. Cut a piece of Fabric #4 to cover the remaining exposed foundation of the left front. Place right side up
   on the foundation and stitch 1/8" from the raw edges.
9. Pin the couched pocket in place on the left jacket
   front with the inner corner next to the corner of the
   Drunkard's Path border. Stitch 1/8" from the raw
   edges.

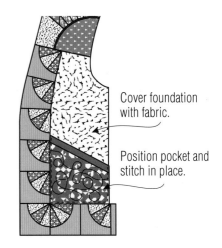

Cover foundation
with fabric.

Position pocket and
stitch in place.

✓Ribbon Weave

MATERIALS

2 yds. each of 4 different colors of ribbon or trim, approximately ¼" wide

Square of synthetic suede large enough to cover upper left front between the pocket and Fandango Fan (approximately 9" square)

1 large decorative button (or pin) and loose beads

DIRECTIONS

1. Cut the suede the size and shape required to cover the space between the bottom edge of Fandango Fan and the top edge of the couched pocket. Divide the piece horizontally into 4 equal sections and cut apart into strips. Pin the strips in place with the raw edges butted to each other. Stitch in place ⅛" from the outer edges to hold the strips in place. Cover the inner raw edges of the Drunkard's Path blocks with trim of your choice. Stitch in place.

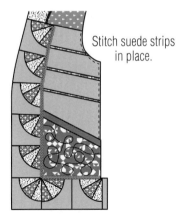

Stitch suede strips in place.

♪ **NOTE:** You may substitute individual strips of suede if you are cutting from scraps.

2. Beginning with the fan on the back of the jacket, position and pin the ribbons on top of the seam lines, bringing the ribbons over the shoulder to the front. On the front, weave the ribbons through the suede strips and pin in place at the bottom edge of the suede.* Some ribbons will end up on top of the bottom strip of suede and some will be underneath it.

The jacket on page 66 shows Ribbon Weave as described in these directions. In the jacket on page 68, the designer decided to end the ribbons on the upper shoulder and anchor them with the large button, rather than weaving them through the suede. To complete the suede area, she cut strips from a second color of synthetic suede to weave in and out of the first set of strips.

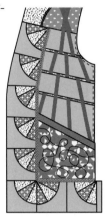

3. Edgestitch the ribbons in place along both finished edges, ending the stitching at the top edge of the upper strip of suede. Sew the large decorative button or pin in place on the jacket front where the ribbons come together. Surround the button with single beads if desired.

4. Add a row of beads and/or braid to anchor the ribbon ends at the edge where Fandango Fan and the suede strips meet.

✓ Tucked Medley

MATERIALS

¼ yd. each of Fabrics #4, #5, #7, and #9
12" x 12" square of lightweight fusible interfacing
⅓ yd. dangling beads
Loose beads

DIRECTIONS

You will need the Perfect Pleater or EZE PLEATER, designed to make ¼"-deep tucks. These tools have stiff, permanent tucks, which are called "louvers."

1. Cut a pocket from the lining fabric. Cut another pocket from a second fabric and position it on the right jacket front with the front and bottom edges next to the Drunkard's Path blocks. Pin in place; stitch ⅛" from all raw edges.

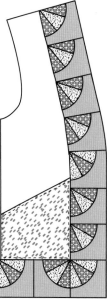

2. Cut a pocket from the square of lightweight fusible interfacing. Make sure the fusible granules are face up as shown below.

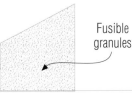

Fusible granules

3. From the fabric you wish to tuck for the finished pocket, cut an 11"-wide strip, cutting across the fabric width from selvage to selvage.

4. Place the pleater on your ironing board with the open edges of the louvers facing away from you. Place the strip of pocket fabric *right side down* on top of the pleater with one short end of the fabric strip parallel to the edge of the pleater.

    Firmly tuck the fabric into each louver, beginning with the one closest to you. Use a very thin metal or plastic ruler or a credit card to push the fabric completely into each louver before making the next tuck. When you have tucked enough fabric to match the length of the pocket pattern piece from top to bottom, apply the pocket cut from fusible interfacing (step 2) to the wrong side of the tucked fabric. Be sure to follow the manufacturer's directions for a permanent fuse. *Allow to cool, then roll the fabric from the pleater.* Trim excess fabric away around the outer edges of the interfacing.

5. Finish the top edge and line the pocket as shown in steps 6 and 7 of Couched Threads on page 76. Add dangling beads below the pocket band. If you have any beads left, you might want to use them to embellish the bottom edge of the Fandango Fan on the jacket back. Set the completed pocket aside.

6. To finish the right jacket front, pleat 2 additional fabrics to cover the remainder of the foundation from the pocket to the shoulder as shown on page 79. See the jacket in the photo on page 66. The other option is to use one or more unpleated fabrics of your choice, choosing ones that help balance the design with the completed left front. This is a particularly appropriate finishing method if you are full busted and prefer not to add additional bulk to the bust area. The jacket on page 68 was finished in this manner.

For pleated pieces:

a. From each of the selected fabrics, cut a 10"-wide strip across the width of the fabric from selvage to selvage.

b. Make tucks in each fabric strip as described for the pocket, in step 4.

c. Add the pleats to the area above the pocket. Place 1 piece in the center of the foundation so that it extends into the armhole area. Pin in place and trim edges even with the foundation and the inner edge of the Drunkard's Path blocks. Stitch $1/8$" from the raw edges.

d. Cut the remaining piece of pleated fabric into 2 pieces to fit the upper shoulder area and the area below the center piece. Pin to the foundation and stitch $1/8$" from the raw edges.

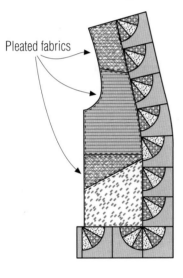

Pleated fabrics

Cover the butted raw edges of the pleated pieces with ribbon or braid, or a string of beads. Embellish the tucks with single beads if desired. Cover the bottom edge of the pleated section with ribbon, or zigzag over the raw edges of the pleated piece and the top edge of the pocket below it to finish the edges.

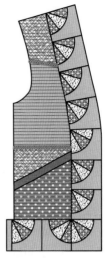

7. Position the tucked pocket on the right front with the lower inner corner next to the corner of the Drunkard's Path border and pin in place. Stitch $1/8$" from raw edges.

8. Cover the inner raw edges of the Drunkard's Path with trim of your choice as you did in step 1 on page 77. Stitch in place.

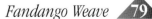

✓Crossroads

MATERIALS

Fabrics #1, #2, #3, #5, #7, and #8

DIRECTIONS

Cut all strips across the width of the fabric from selvage to selvage.

1. From each of the fabrics, cut 2 strips, each $1^1/_2$" wide. Make 2 identical strip-pieced units, using 1 strip of each fabric in each unit. Use $^1/_4$"-wide seams and press all seams in each unit in one direction. Each strip-pieced unit should be $6^1/_2$" x 42"–44".

2. Using a 45° x 90° right-angle triangle, cut each strip-pieced unit into 6 triangles for a total of 12. Rotate the triangle with each cut as shown. Each triangle will measure approximately $8^1/_2$" on the two short sides.

♪ **NOTE:** It may be necessary to sew the short piece cut from the first end of the unit to the other short end, to get the sixth triangle from the strip-pieced unit. Match seams carefully.

3. Fold the right sleeve foundation in half and press to make a crease down the center.

Right sleeve

4. Place triangles on the sleeve foundation and move them around to create a pleasing arrangement. Keep the design symmetrical as shown in the sample designs below.

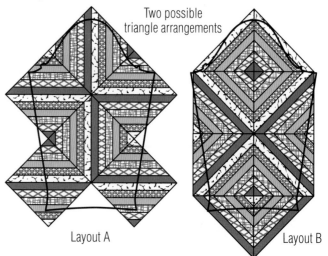

Two possible triangle arrangements

Layout A   Layout B

5. Sew triangles together in the desired arrangement. Sew sets of triangles together to make the required squares or triangles and then sew the squares together in rows.

OR

6. Pin the completed patchwork in position on the sleeve, using the crease to help you center it. Trim the outer edges even with the sleeve foundation.

7. Stitch $^1/_4$" from all outer edges. Use small cutaway pieces to fill in uncovered foundation areas.

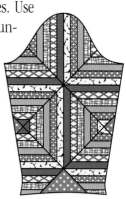

✓Bias Binding

MATERIALS

½ yd. fabric

DIRECTIONS

1. Open out the fabric and turn down one corner to form a triangle. Cut along the fold line.

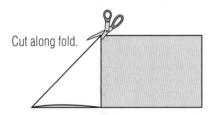
Cut along fold.

2. With right sides together, sew the cutaway triangle to the opposite end of the fabric, using a ¼"-wide seam allowance. Press the seam open.

3. Position a ruler for a cut 3" from the diagonal edge and make a 1"-long mark on each long edge of the fabric. Continue marking across the remainder of the fabric in 3" increments. *At the top edge of the strip, label the first 1"-long mark Point 1. On the bottom edge, label the second mark Point 2. Rotary cut between the marks, leaving each 1" marked section uncut.*

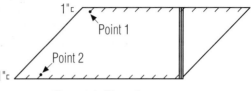
1"⌐
Point 1
Point 2
1"⌐
Space cuts 3" apart.

4. Fold the cut strip in half lengthwise, right sides together, and match Point 1 to Point 2. Pin until you have formed a spiral cylinder of fabric strips. Stitch, using a ¼"-wide seam allowance.

5. Cut the cylinder open across the seam to form one continuous strip of bias binding. Press seams open.

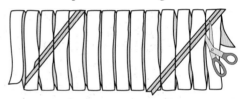

6. Fold the continuous binding strip in half, wrong sides together, and press, being careful not to stretch it.

✓ *Jacket Finishing*

1. With right sides together, stitch the right front to the jacket back at the shoulder. Press the seam open. Stitch the lining back to the fronts at the shoulders and press the seams open.

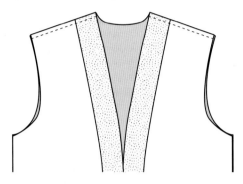

2. Finish all raw edges of the patchwork pieces on the jacket and sleeves with your choice of gimp, braid, or bias binding as shown in step 6 on page 16.
3. Compare the completed patchwork jacket and sleeves to the lining pieces as shown in step 9 on page 17. Trim as necessary.
4. Complete steps 10–12 on page 17.
5. Complete step 13 on page 17, ending the stitching at the dot for the slit. Press the seam open, continuing to press under ½" at the slit opening. Repeat for the lining, turning under ⅝" along slit opening edges.

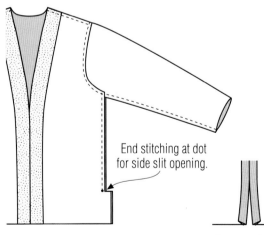

End stitching at dot for side slit opening.

Press under ½" at slit opening.

♪ NOTE: If you do not want side slits, you can sew the seams all the way to the bottom edge of the jacket and the lining.

6. Complete step 14 on page 17.
7. Try on the jacket *with the shoulder pads pinned in place* from the outside. Adjust shoulder pad placement as needed. Check sleeve length. You will bind the bottom edges of the sleeves so they should be the correct length at this point. If they are too long, trim away excess at the bottom edges and do the same at the bottom edges of the sleeve linings.
8. Sew the shoulder pads in place as shown in step 15 on page 17.
9. Place the lining inside the jacket with *wrong sides together* and raw edges matching. Pin in place. Slipstitch lining edges to slit seam allowances.

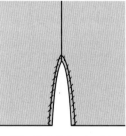

Slipstitch lining to slit.

♪ NOTE: If you would prefer to bind the slit edges, as shown in the directions in the box at right, cut away the slit seam allowance in the jacket and the lining. Treat the raw edges of the seam allowances above the slit with a seam sealant, such as Fray Check™.

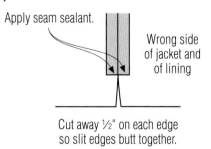

Apply seam sealant.

Wrong side of jacket and of lining

Cut away ½" on each edge so slit edges butt together.

10. Bind the neckline and bottom edges of the jacket and the bottom edges of the sleeves, following the binding instructions in the box below. If you wish, you may bind the bottom edges only, or you may bind the slit edges as well. See directions for both methods below and on page 84.

♪ **NOTE:** If you have an even-feed foot for your sewing maching, use it when sewing binding to the edges of your jacket.

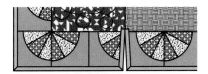

Bind the slit.

OR

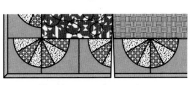

Bind bottom edges only.

To bind the bottom and slit edges:

1. Open out the binding and turn under ¼" on one short end. Press and refold.

Turn under ¼".

2. Beginning at the top of one slit opening edge, pin the binding to the jacket with right sides together, ending the pinning ½" from the bottom edge of the jacket. Allow at least ¼" of binding to extend above the point when the slit begins. Stitch ½" from the raw edges, ending the stitching ½" above the bottom corner of the slit.

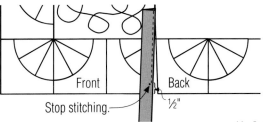

Front   Back

Stop stitching.   ½"

3. Fold the binding back on itself, creating a 45° angle. The binding should form a straight line with the bottom edge of the jacket.

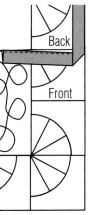

Back

Front

Hold the fold in place with your finger and fold the rest of the binding back over itself, even with the jacket edge. Pin in place. Stitch, beginning at the corner edge. Repeat these steps at each remaining corner, ending at the upper edge of the remaining front slit.

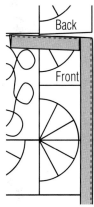

Back

Front

Turn the binding to the inside and slipstitch in place, folding a miter in each corner.

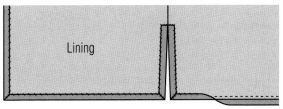

Lining

Slipstitch in place.

Bind the slit edges and the bottom edge of the back in the same manner.

To bind the bottom edge only:

1. Prepare the binding as shown in step 1 on page 83.
2. Beginning at the bottom edge of the jacket at one slit edge, pin the binding to the jacket with raw edges even. Stitch ½" from the raw edges, mitering the corners as shown on page 83.

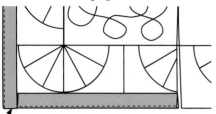

— Miter corner here.

3. Turn the binding to the inside and slipstitch in place as shown on page 83.

To bind the sleeve edges:

1. Open out the binding and turn under one edge at a 45° angle as shown. Trim, leaving a ¼"-wide seam allowance. Refold.

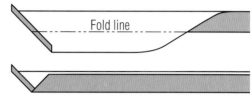

Fold line

2. With right sides together, pin the binding to the sleeve edge, beginning and ending somewhere near but not exactly at the underarm seam as shown, to avoid bulk in the seam area. Cut away excess binding and tuck the end into the beginning of the bias. Stitch ½" from the raw edges, then turn binding to the inside and slipstitch in place as shown on page 83.

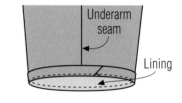

Underarm seam

Lining

Jacket Nine by Dora Conner, Beaumont, Texas. Dora used a sparkling butterfly pin to anchor free floating ribbons in this jacket variation.

Dora created an illusion of reflected light with careful placement of color and contrast in the dramatic fan.

Waltz Across Texas

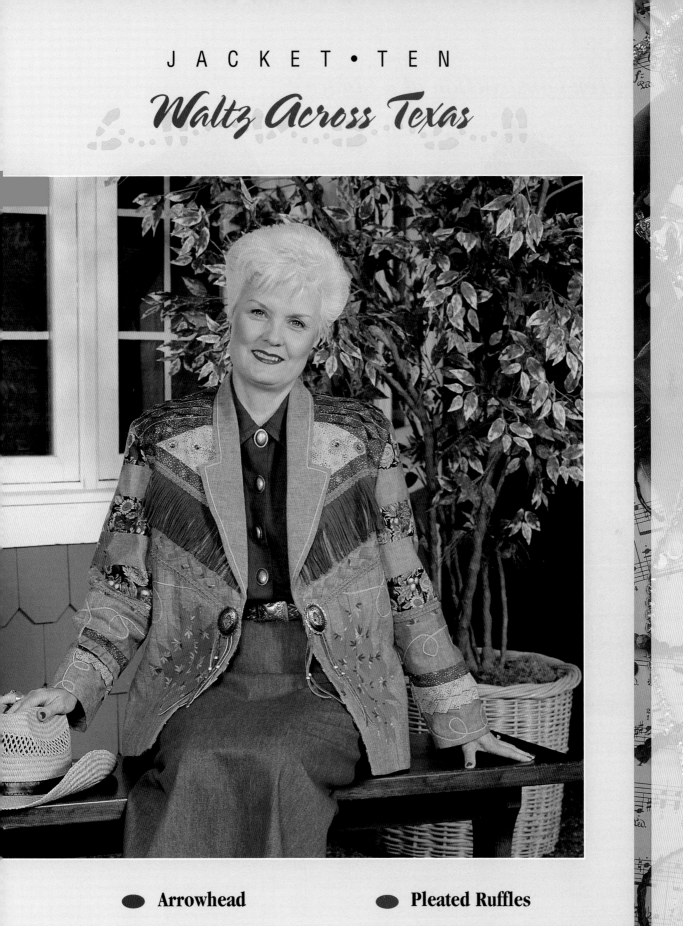

- ● Arrowhead
- ● Monster Mash
- ● Seminole Stroll
- ● Pleated Ruffles
- ● Blazing Star

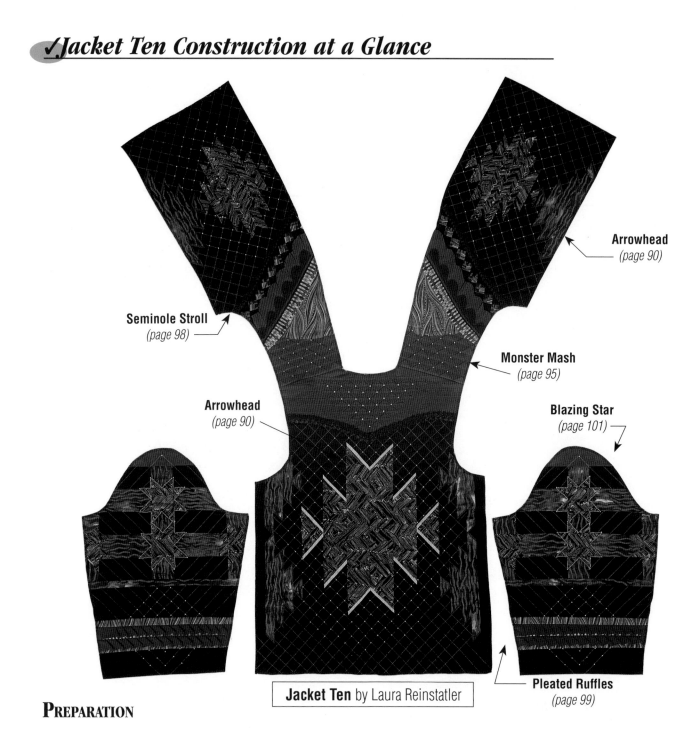

Arrowhead
(page 90)

Seminole Stroll
(page 98)

Monster Mash
(page 95)

Arrowhead
(page 90)

Blazing Star
(page 101)

Jacket Ten by Laura Reinstatler

Pleated Ruffles
(page 99)

PREPARATION

1. Cut the jacket back, fronts, and sleeves from the foundation fabric and from the lining. Cut lightweight fusible interfacing, using the front and back neckline facing pattern pieces for Jacket 10. Set the lining pieces aside.

2. Following the manufacturer's directions, apply the fusible interfacing to the wrong side of the jacket front and back foundation pieces. Set the fronts and sleeves aside.

3. Trace the yoke placement line onto the right side of the foundation back.

Apply interfacing to both foundation fronts.

Apply interfacing to the back neckline.

Trace yoke placement line.

Shopping List

All yardage requirements are based on 44"-wide fabrics, unless otherwise noted. When using the same fabric for more than one patchwork technique, combine the yardage requirements.

Jacket Foundation	2½ yds. cotton flannel or muslin*
Jacket Lining	2½ yds. silky lining fabric or smooth cotton fabric
Interfacing	½ yd. lightweight fusible interfacing
Shoulder Pads	Raglan-style shoulder pads
Arrowhead	1⅓ yds. Fabric A (solid)
	½ yd. Fabric #1
	⅓ yd. Fabric #2
Monster Mash	⅔ yd. Fabric #3
	⅛ yd. Wonder-Under or Fine Fuse
Seminole Stroll	1"-wide strip of Fabric A**
	1½"-wide strip of Fabric #1**
	3"-wide strip of Fabric #2**
Pleated Ruffles	¼ yd. Fabric A (solid)
	⅛ yd. Fabric #3
	¼ yd. Fabric #5
	Leftover lightweight fusible interfacing
Blazing Star	¼ yd. each of Fabrics A, #1, and #4
Buttons	4 decorative buttons, ½" diameter
Conchos	2 in size of your choice
Decorative Braid	3 yds. to cover seams
Narrow Trim	Soutache braid or other ⅛"- to ¼"-wide flexible trim to make stitched loops (optional)
Fringe	⅔ yd. in type and length of your choice***
Leather strips (¼" wide)	2½ yds.***

  * Preshrink the foundation fabric, allow to dry, and press to remove wrinkles.
 ** Cut strips across the fabric width from selvage to selvage.
*** You can rotary cut these from real suede or leather or from a synthetic suede, such as UltraSuede®.

In addition to the fabrics and notions listed, you will need the following special supplies:

45° x 90° triangle, at least 8" tall
Perfect Pleater or EZE PLEATER
Chalk pencil or soap sliver
Tuck and Point Guide
Optional: Tricot foot for your machine (This foot has a hole in front to hold the trim as you stitch. It makes it easier to control the trim.)

FABRIC SELECTION TIPS

- Choose 1 solid and 5 prints for a total of 6 fabrics. Choose prints in a variety of scales—tiny, small, medium, medium-large, and large.
- You need a total of 2 yards of the solid for the basic background fabric. Identify this as Fabric A.
- In addition, you need a total of ⅔ yard each of 3 prints (Fabrics #1, #2, and #3) and ½ yard each of 2 additional prints (Fabrics #4 and #5).
- For easy reference, make a swatch card containing a piece of each and label with the appropriate identification letter or number.

✓Arrowhead

MATERIALS

1⅓ yds. Fabric A
½ yd. Fabric #1
⅓ yd. Fabric #2
Narrow trim (or soutache)

DIRECTIONS

Cut all strips across the width of the fabric from selvage to selvage.

To make the arrowheads, you will need a 45° x 90° triangle for cutting triangles.

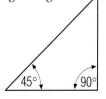

Jacket Back

1. From Fabric A, cut 2 strips, each 9" wide. Trim each strip to a length of 32". Place the strips right sides together and cut in half with a 45°-angle cut. You will then have 4 strips, each with a long edge that measures 20½".

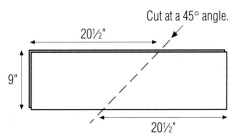

Cut at a 45° angle.
20½"
9"
20½"

2. From Fabric #1, cut 1 strip, 9" wide. From this strip, cut two 45° triangles.

3. Sew a strip of Fabric A (from step 1) to each short side of each triangle. Offset the ends ¼" as shown and stitch ¼" from the raw edges. Press seams away from the triangle.

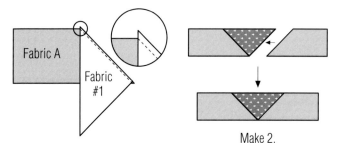

Fabric A
Fabric #1
Make 2.

4. Cut each pieced unit into 3"-wide strips.

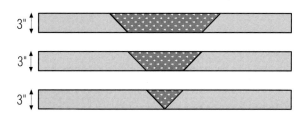

3"
3"
3"

5. Arrange the strips as shown below to create the Arrowhead design. Pin strips together, working from the center out and making sure that the design doesn't shift out of position. Sew the strips together, using ¼"-wide seam allowances. Press the two outermost seams toward the center and the remaining seams all in the same direction.

Press in direction of arrows.

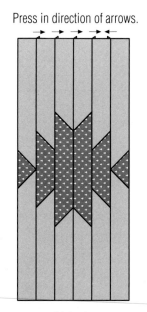

Make 1.

6. Place the completed Arrowhead section on the foundation back so that the points at the top are 1" below the yoke line. Pin in place and trim even with the yoke line and the bottom edge of the foundation back. Save the pieces you trim away.

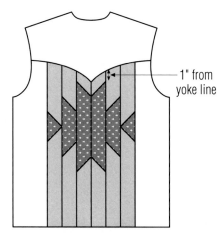

1" from yoke line

7. To make the Arrowhead sections for the left and right of the center Arrowhead, cut 1 strip, 6" wide, from Fabric A. With the 42"-long strip folded in half, cut along the fold, then make a 45° cut as shown so that the long edge of each resulting piece measures 14". You will have a total of 4 pieces, each with an angled end and a straight end.

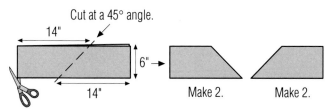

Cut at a 45° angle.

14"

6"

14"

Make 2.   Make 2.

8. From Fabric #2, cut 1 strip, 6" wide. Open out the strip and cut four 45° triangles, each 6" tall.

6"

Cut 4 triangles.

9. From Fabric A, cut 1 strip, 6" wide. Open out the strip and cut two 45° triangles, each 6" tall.

6"

Cut 2 triangles.

10. Make 2 pieced units as shown. Stitch the pieces together, using ¼"-wide seam allowances and offsetting the seams as shown in step 3 above.

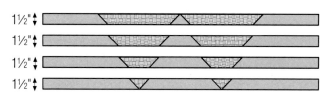

Make 2.

11. Cut each pieced unit into 4 strips, each 1½" wide.

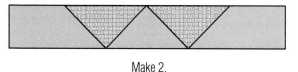

1½"
1½"
1½"
1½"

12. To make the half-Arrowhead units for the side back areas of the jacket, arrange the strips as shown below. Sew the strips together, using ¼"-wide seam allowances. Press all seams toward the wider points.

Press.

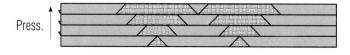

13. Position a half-Arrowhead unit at each side of the Arrowhead on the back foundation, taking care to center the design. If it does not cover the entire foundation out to the side seam, you can add an extra strip of background fabric at the underarm section or you can add it next to the center Arrowhead. *Decide now how you will handle this.*

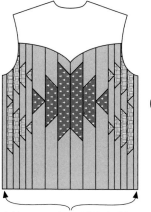   OR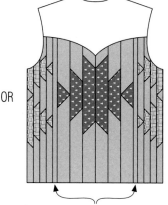

Add extra strips of Fabric A here.   Add extra strips of Fabric A here.

To attach the half-Arrowhead (or the extra back-ground strip) to the foundation, turn each unit onto the center Arrowhead with right sides together. With raw edges even, stitch ¼" from them through all layers, ending the stitching at the yoke line on the foundation. Flip back onto the foundation, press, and pin in place.

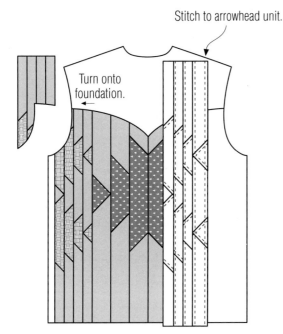

Turn onto foundation.

Stitch to arrowhead unit.

14. Trim the half-Arrowhead units even with the arm-hole edges and the yoke line. Set aside the armhole cutaway sections to use on the sleeves. Trim the bot-tom edge even with the foundation. Add a strip of Fabric A to each side, if necessary, to cover any exposed foundation at the underarms. Stitch the strips in place and flip onto the foundation as you did the half-Arrowheads. Stitch ⅛" from the upper edge and ¼" from remaining raw edges to secure the Arrow-head and half-Arrowhead units to the foundation.

Optional: Arrange soutache braid in a loop de-sign between the Arrowheads on each side. (See the jacket photo on page 86.) I used the handle of my dress shears as a pattern. Stitch by machine, using a braid or tricot foot to hold the trim as you stitch.

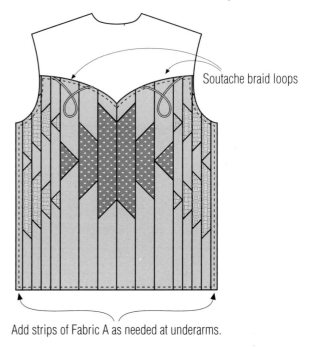

Soutache braid loops

Add strips of Fabric A as needed at underarms.

Jacket Fronts

1. From Fabric A, cut 3 strips, each 6" wide. With strips still folded, make one 45° cut in the center of each. Cut along the fold of each strip. You will have mirror-image sets of 6 pieces each for a total of 12 pieces.

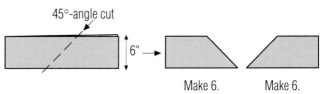

45°-angle cut

6"

Make 6.   Make 6.

2. From Fabric #1, cut 1 strip, 6" wide. Open the strip and cut four 45° triangles.

6"

Cut 4 triangles.

3. Using 4 mirror-image sets cut in step 1 on page 92, and 4 triangles cut in step 2 on page 92, make 4 pieced units as shown. Use $1/4$"-wide seam allowances and offset the pieces for each seam as shown in step 3 for the jacket back on page 90.

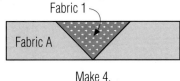

Make 4.

4. Cut each pieced unit into 4 strips, each $1^1/2$" wide.

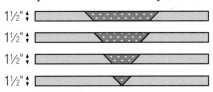

5. Reposition the strips as shown and sew together, using $1/4$"-wide seam allowances to make 2 complete Arrowheads, 1 for each of the lower center fronts of the jacket. Press the seams in one direction in each unit. Set aside for the center fronts.

Make 2.

6. From Fabric #2, cut 1 strip, 6" wide. Open the strip and cut two 45° triangles.

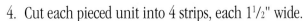

Cut 2 triangles.

7. Using the remaining mirror-image sets cut in step 1 on page 92, and triangles cut in step 2 on page 92, make 2 pieced units. Sew the pieces together, using $1/4$"-wide seams and offsetting the ends as shown in step 3 for the jacket back on page 91.

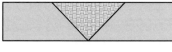

Make 2.

8. Cut each pieced unit into 4 strips, each $1^1/2$" wide.

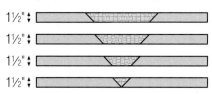

9. Arrange the strips as shown and stitch together, using $1/4$"-wide seam allowances to make 2 identical half-Arrowheads. Press seams in the direction indicated by the arrows.

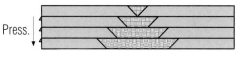

Press.

Make 2.

10. Place the jacket back foundation (with Arrowhead) on a flat surface with a jacket front foundation at each side. Position a half-Arrowhead on each jacket front in line with the half-Arrowheads on the jacket back. Remember that there may be a strip of background fabric at the jacket back underarm that will split this design. Pin in place.

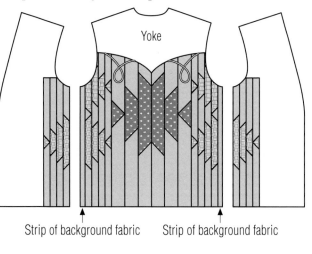

Yoke

Strip of background fabric   Strip of background fabric

11. Position an Arrowhead on each jacket front, setting it just below the last point of the side half-Arrowhead as shown. Turn the Arrowhead face down on the half-Arrowhead and stitch through all layers 1/4" from the raw edges. Flip back onto the foundation, press, and pin in place. If necessary, add a strip of background fabric at center front to cover the foundation. Trim the outer edges of the Arrowhead even with the foundation. *Do not trim the top edge at the yoke line yet.* Stitch 1/4" from the outer raw edges to anchor the patchwork to the foundation.

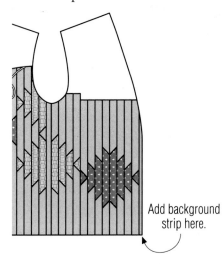

Add background strip here.

♪ **NOTE:** If you prefer, you may position the Arrowheads in line with the half-Arrowheads as was done in the jacket in the photo on page 88.

This design was adapted with permission from Nancy Brenan Daniel, who featured the Arrowhead technique in her booklet "Delectable Mountains." For more information on using this quick-piecing technique, contact Brenan Daniel Publishing, 2057 East Malibu Drive, Tempe, Arizona 85282.

✓*Monster Mash*
(Better known as Shark's Teeth)

MATERIALS

²/₃ yd. Fabric #3
Scrap of Fabric #2
Scrap of Fabric A (solid)
¹/₈ yd. Wonder-Under or Fine Fuse

DIRECTIONS

Back Yoke

1. From Fabric #3, cut a 20" x 22" piece. Using a chalk pencil or soap sliver, draw a line 2¹/₂" above the lower long edge on the *right side* of the fabric. Mark 6 more lines, each 2¹/₄" apart. This will make tucks that are ³/₄" deep. You will not make tucks in the upper portion of the yoke. (This avoids having "dinosaur points" standing at attention on your shoulders!)

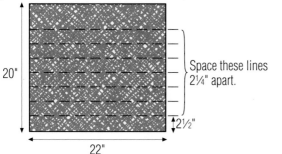

2. Place the marked fabric *wrong side* up on the ironing board. Carefully fold and press along each chalk line, *wrong sides* together.
3. Stitch ³/₄" from each fold line. It's important that this stitching is straight and accurate.
4. Press all tucks toward the bottom edge of the piece, which will become the bottom edge of the back yoke.

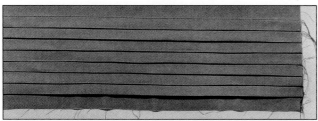

5. With a chalk pencil or a soap sliver, draw a line down the center of the tucks, perpendicular to the stitching.
6. Trace the back yoke shape for your size onto tissue paper and cut out. Place the tissue paper yoke on top of the tucked piece with the center line on the yoke point and trace the yoke onto the tucked fabric, using a soap sliver or a marking pencil that will show on your fabric.

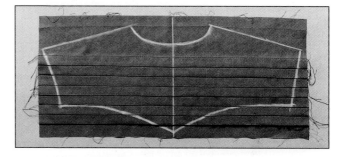

7. Starting with the bottom tuck, place Tuck and Point guide on the tuck aligning a dot of the guide with the center mark on the tucked fabric. Make sure you are using the correct side of the guide for the ³/₄" tuck.

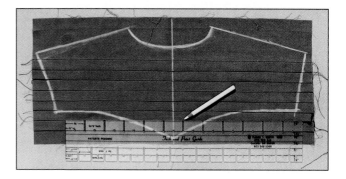

8. Make marks at the guide slits for each point desired. (The dots are the center of each point.) Use the yoke pattern as a guide for determining point location. Mark only 1 point on the lowest tuck, 2 on the next, then additional ones as you move up the piece. Stagger the tuck location as you move up the fabric piece. To stagger, place the guide on top of each tuck, matching the lines with the points of the previous row. Experiment with skipping areas to make sections of a row without points. You will be surprised at the interesting patterns you can create with this technique. (See the photos on pages 88 and 105 for point layouts.)

9. After marking each point, cut up to, but not through, the stitching on each marked line.

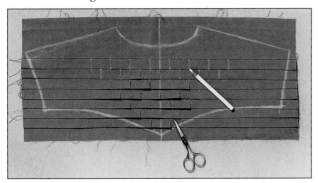

10. At the ironing board, hold the tucked piece so that the underside of each tuck shows. Fold the corner of each slashed edge under toward the stitching, forming a triangle. Be sure the point of the triangle is true and not squared off at the tip. Use a straight pin to hold the point to the ironing board. Place a snip of Fine Fuse or Wonder-Under (without the paper) under the triangle and press. Press all completed tucks and points flat.

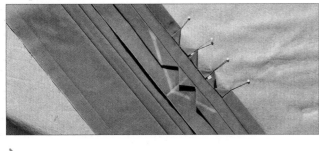

♪ **NOTE:** Add a bead to each completed point if desired. See the jacket in the photo on page 88.

11. From the right side, triple straight-stitch $^1/_{32}$" away from each original row of tuck stitching, or substitute a narrow zigzag or other decorative stitch if you wish. This stitching catches the raw edge of each triangle under the tuck.

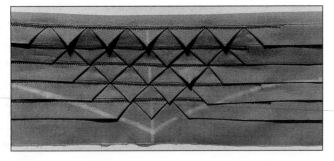

12. Cut out the yoke on the lines marked in step 6. Place the yoke in position above the Arrowhead on the jacket back. Stitch $^1/_8$" from the yoke edge and $^1/_4$" from all remaining raw edges. Use braid or other trim to cover the raw edges where the Monster Mash and Arrowhead meet. Some of my students have added fringe here, too, but be aware that fringe will cover up the top points of the Arrowhead.

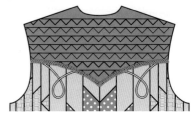

Front Yokes

1. From Fabric #3, cut 2 pieces, each 11" x 20$^1/_2$". On each piece, draw a line 2$^1/_4$" below the short edge on the *right side* of the fabric. Draw additional lines 2$^1/_4$" apart until you reach the lower edge and there is only 1$^1/_4$" of unmarked fabric left. Make tucks in the same manner as for the back yoke.

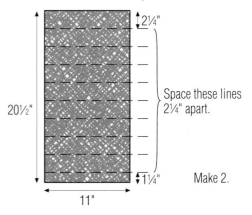

2. Trace the *upper section* of the front yoke pattern for your size onto tissue paper and cut out. Arrange the tissue-paper pattern on the tucked fabric and trace around it, using a soap sliver or a marking pencil that will show on your fabric.

3. Mark and make points in each piece in the same manner as shown for the back yoke.

4. Position the tissue-paper pattern for the upper yoke section on the completed Monster Mash and *cut out a left and right upper front yoke.* Position each yoke on the foundation, pin in place, and stitch $^1/_8$"

from the bottom edge and ¼" from all remaining raw edges.

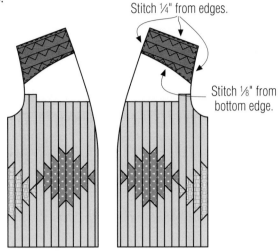

Stitch ¼" from edges.

Stitch ⅛" from bottom edge.

5. Trace the *lower section* of the front yoke for your size onto tissue paper and add ¼"-wide seam allowances on the top and outer edges as shown to make a pattern.

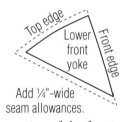

Top edge
Lower front yoke
Front edge
Add ¼"-wide seam allowances.

6. Use the *lower section* of the front yoke pattern piece to cut a fill-in piece for each front from Fabric #2. Place the top edge of the piece right sides together at the bottom edge of the upper section of the yoke. Stitch ¼" from the raw edges through all layers. Turn down onto the foundation, press, and pin. Stitch ¼" from the front edge and ⅛" from the inner edge.

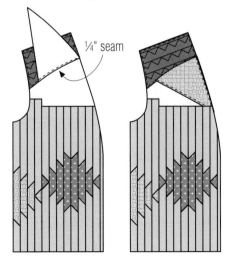

¼" seam

7. Cut a 1½"-wide strip of Fabric #3 and with right sides together, stitch to the bottom edge of the lower yoke. Turn down onto the foundation and press. Stitch ⅛" from the raw edge. Cut a strip of Fabric A the width of your fringe plus ½". Stitch to the bottom edge of the strip of Fabric #3 in the same manner. Turn down, press, and stitch ⅛" from the lower edge. Later, you will add a strip of Seminole Stroll, which will finish to 1¼" wide. You will add the fringe (and decorative braid if desired) after completing the fronts.

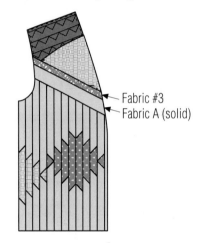

Fabric #3
Fabric A (solid)

♪ **NOTE:** Study the already-placed front Arrowhead pieces as you place each of these strips. You may need to adjust the strip widths to fill the area completely.

✓ Seminole Stroll

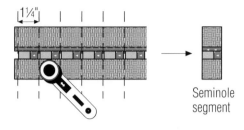

Seminole segment

MATERIALS

1½"-wide strip of Fabric #1
3"-wide strip of Fabric #2
1"-wide strip of Fabric A

DIRECTIONS

Cut all strips across the width of the fabric from selvage to selvage.

1. Cut the Fabric #1 strip in half lengthwise to form 2 long strips, each ¾" wide. Do the same with the Fabric #2 strip, creating 2 strips, each 1½" wide.

2. Sew the Fabric A strip to a Fabric #1 strip, using a ¼"-wide seam. Press seam toward darker fabric. Crosscut the strip-pieced unit into 1"-wide segments.

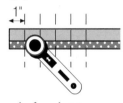

3. Stitch a short end of each 1" segment to a 1½"-wide strip of Fabric #2 as shown. The segment edges should just touch each other without overlapping. Press the seam toward the strip-pieced segments.

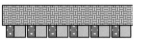

4. Stitch the remaining strip of Fabric #1 to the remaining strip of Fabric #2. Press the seam toward the darker fabric.

5. Sew the resulting unit to the other edge of the 1" segments as shown. Press the seam toward the strip-pieced unit. Cut into 1¼" segments, cutting between the 1" segments.

6. Offset the segments and chain-stitch together in pairs. Then chain-stitch the pairs together. Continue chain-stitching all units together to create a finished piece approximately 42" long. Trim away and discard the "rooftops" as shown, cutting ¼" away from the corners of the pieced squares in the strips. You may want to mark a cutting line, then use your scissors to cut on the line. I find this more accurate than using a rotary cutter for this step.

Trim away "rooftops."

7. Place the completed Seminole strip face down on a jacket front, aligning a raw edge with the bottom edge of the background strip. Holding the Arrowhead patchwork out of the way, stitch ¼" from the edge, turn down onto the foundation, press, and pin in place. Trim the excess Seminole strip even with the front and side edges. Stitch ¼" from all raw edges. Repeat on the remaining jacket front. Trim the top edge of the Arrowhead even with the lower edge of the Seminole strip on each jacket front. Stitch ⅛" from the raw edge. Cover the raw edges with the braid or trim of your choice. Stitch the fringe in place on the background strip below the yoke. Arrange and stitch soutache braid in loops on the fronts between the Arrowheads if desired.

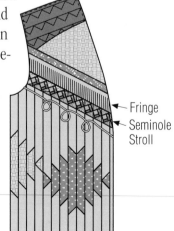

Fringe
Seminole Stroll

✓Pleated Ruffles

You will need the Perfect Pleater or EZE PLEATER, designed to make ¹/₄"-deep tucks. These tools have stiff, permanent tucks, called "louvers."

MATERIALS

¹/₄ yd. Fabric A
¹/₈ yd. Fabric #3
¹/₄ yd. Fabric #5
¹/₄"-wide strips of lightweight fusible interfacing

DIRECTIONS

Cut all strips across the width of the fabric from selvage to selvage.

1. From Fabric A, cut 2 strips, each 5" wide.

   ♪ **NOTE:** You can use the strip-pieced leftovers cut from the top and bottom edges of the Arrowhead pieces if you wish.

   From Fabric #3, cut 2 strips, each 1¹/₂" wide. From Fabric #5, cut 2 strips, each 3¹/₂" wide.

2. Fold each strip of Fabric #5 in half lengthwise, *wrong sides together*. Press. Cut each piece into 2 equal lengths for a total of 4 folded strips.

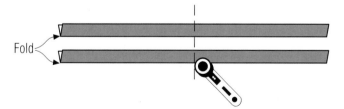

3. Place the pleater on the ironing board with the open edges of the louvers facing away from you. Place one end of one of the folded strips at an angle in the far left corner of the pleater board so that you will be forming pleats diagonally across the pleater. With your fingers, tuck the strip into the first tuck. Repeat this step in every third louver until you reach the end of the board. Steam-press the pleats in place while in the pleater.

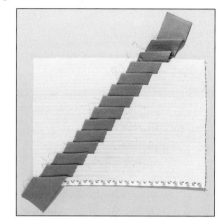

4. With the fabric still in the pleater, apply a ¹/₄"-wide strip of fusible interfacing to the strip near the raw edges. Allow the strip to cool and roll it out of the pleater. Repeat with the remaining Fabric #5 strips.

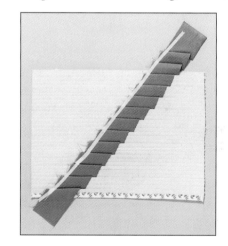

   ♪ **NOTE:** If your pleater is not wide enough to accommodate the length of the fabric strip, remove the fused strip and insert the unpleated section into the pleater at the left-hand corner. Continue pleating.

5. Machine stitch through the interfacing and trim the raw edges of the pleats even with the top edge of the interfacing strip.

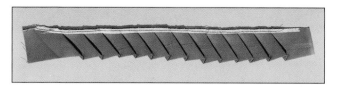

6. If you prefer to make the "Alternate Sleeve Design" shown on page 102 instead of 2 identical sleeves, complete the following steps on only one of the sleeve foundations. (Both completed sleeves are shown at the bottom of page 102.) Set two ruffle strips aside for the alternate sleeve.

   From Fabric A, cut a 5"-wide strip long enough to fit across the bottom edge of each sleeve. Position a strip on each sleeve foundation with the lower edges even. Pin in place, trim outer edges even with the foundation, and stitch ¼" from side and lower edges.

7. Place one pleated ruffle on top of Fabric A with raw edges even. Stitch ⅛" from the raw edges through all layers.

Ruffle

Fabric A

8. With right sides together, position a 1½"-wide strip of Fabric #3 on top of the ruffle with raw edges even. Stitch ¼" from the raw edges, turn up the Fabric #3 strip onto the foundation, press, and pin in place. Trim outer edges even with the foundation.

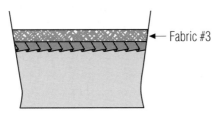

Fabric #3

9. Place a second ruffle on top of the Fabric #3 strip, keeping raw edges even. Stitch ⅛" from the raw edges through all layers.

   Set the sleeves aside until you have completed the Blazing Star patchwork on page 101.

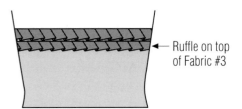

Ruffle on top of Fabric #3

10. Repeat step 8, adding another strip of Fabric #3 above the second ruffle.

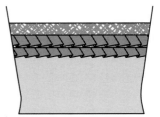

✓Blazing Star

MATERIALS

¼ yd. each of Fabrics A, #1, and #4

DIRECTIONS

1. From Fabric A, cut:
   - 8 rectangles, each 2¾" x 6"
   - 14 squares, each 2¾" x 2¾"

2. From Fabric #1, cut:
   - 8 squares, each 2¾" x 2¾"
   - 56 squares, each 1⅝" x 1⅝"

3. From Fabric #4, cut:
   - 12 rectangles, each 2¾" x 6"

4. Place a 1⅝" Fabric #1 square in a corner of each of the Fabric A rectangles, with right sides together and raw edges even. Stitch diagonally from corner to corner. (Mark a diagonal stitching line, or if you prefer, stitch without a line, following the illustrations in the note with step 3 for the Black Tie patchwork on page 55.)

   Stitch.

5. Cut away the corner on each, leaving a ¼"-wide seam allowance beyond the stitching. Turn the remaining triangle toward the seam and press.

   Cut.

6. Repeat steps 4 and 5 on the other corner at the same short end of each Fabric A rectangle. Add squares to the remaining 2 corners on 4 of these rectangles.

   Make 4.   Make 4.

7. Add 2 squares to one end of 12 of the Fabric A squares and add 4 squares to each of the 2 remaining squares of Fabric A in the same manner.

   Make 12.   Make 2.

8. Assemble a Blazing Star unit for each sleeve as shown below, using the pieced squares and rectangles and the 2¾" x 6" rectangles of Fabric #4. Sew the pieces together in horizontal rows, then sew the rows together, matching the seams.

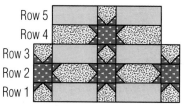

Row 5
Row 4
Row 3
Row 2
Row 1

Make 2.

COMPLETING THE SLEEVES

If you are making identical sleeves, complete them in the following manner. If not, use the alternate design on page 102 for the second sleeve.

1. Place a Blazing Star patchwork piece on the sleeve. Adjust the position so that Row #5 of the patchwork comes almost to the top of the sleeve cap and the top star is completely on the foundation. Some foundation will show above the patchwork.

   Cut a 5"-wide strip of Fabric A to fit between the bottom edge of the Blazing Star and the top edge of the upper ruffle. Add a strip of Fabric #1 below Blazing Star if the strip of Fabric A does not cover the sleeve foundation.

2. With right sides together, stitch the bottom edge of the strip of Fabric A to the top edge of the upper ruffle. Turn up onto the foundation, pin, trim, and stitch ¼" from the outer edges. Repeat with the Blazing Star. Add a strip of Fabric #1 (the same fabric used for the Seminole Stroll) at the top of the sleeve to cover the remaining foundation.

3. Embellish the strips of Fabric A above and below the ruffles with swirls of soutache braid if desired. Topstitch in place.

   Add strip of Fabric 1 here.

   Row 5

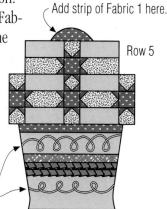

   Soutache braid

ALTERNATE SLEEVE DESIGN

(as seen in the jacket on page 105)

MATERIALS

Two Arrowhead leftovers from jacket back
Two ruffle strips set aside in step 6, page 100
¼ yd. each, Fabrics A and #1

DIRECTIONS

1. Sew the long edges of the Arrowhead leftovers together, using a ¼"-wide seam allowance. Press the seam in one direction.

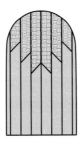

2. Fold the remaining sleeve foundation in half lengthwise at the shoulder dot and crease. Place the Arrowhead piece in the center of the sleeve toward the bottom edge. Position so that the center seam is in line with the crease in the sleeve. Align the top curved edge of the Arrowhead piece with the top edge of the upper strip of background Fabric A on the completed Blazing Star sleeve. Add 5"-wide strips of Fabric A to the right and left of Arrowhead piece, with bottom edges even. Stitch a strip to each side, turn onto the foundation, press, pin in place, and trim even with the edges of the foundation. Stitch ¼" from the outer raw edges.

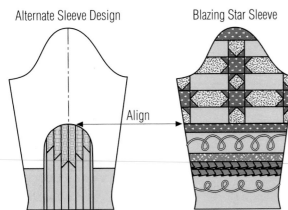

Alternate Sleeve Design   Blazing Star Sleeve

Align

3. Add Fabric #3 ruffles and strips to the right and left of the Arrowhead piece in the same manner as described for the first sleeve (page 100). Turn under the raw edges over the edge of the Arrowhead as you go and edgestitch in place.

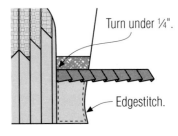

Turn under ¼".

Edgestitch.

4. Add 5"-wide strips of Fabric A to finish covering the foundation to match the first sleeve, turning under the edges and covering the raw edges of the Arrowhead piece. Edgestitch in place. Add the Blazing Star patchwork and then a strip of Fabric #1 at the top of the sleeve, as you did for the first sleeve (page 101).

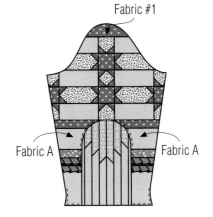

Fabric #1

Fabric A   Fabric A

5. Topstitch soutache braid around the curve of the Arrowhead to cover the stitching and embellish the edge. Add more soutache as desired.

Add soutache braid embellishment.

✓ Jacket Finishing

1. Embellish the completed patchwork pieces with additional trim if desired. For example, beading and quilting in metallic thread were added to the front, back, and sleeves of the jacket in the photo on page 88.

2. With right sides together, stitch the patchwork fronts to the patchwork back at the shoulders as shown in step 8 on page 16. Press seams open. Repeat with the lining pieces.

3. Compare the completed patchwork jacket and sleeves to the lining pieces as shown in step 9 on page 17. Trim as necessary.

4. Cut 4 collars from Fabric A (solid). Cut 2 collars from lightweight fusible interfacing. Apply the interfacing to the wrong side of 2 of the collar pieces.

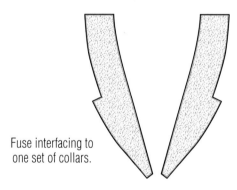

Fuse interfacing to one set of collars.

5. With right sides together, stitch the center back seam of the interfaced collar pieces. Repeat with the remaining collar pieces. Trim the seams to $1/4$" and press open.

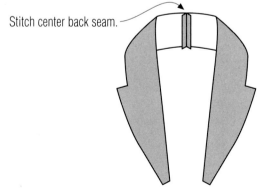

Stitch center back seam.

6. With right sides together, pin the interfaced collar to the neck edge of the jacket lining, matching the center back seam in the collar to the center back of the lining. Stitch $1/2$" from raw edges. Repeat with the

patchwork jacket and the remaining collar. Trim each neckline seam to $1/4$" and press open.

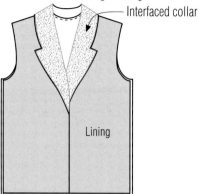

Interfaced collar

Lining

7. Sew the patchwork sleeves to the patchwork jacket and the lining sleeves to the lining jacket, following steps 10–12 on page 17.

8. Stitch the side and sleeve seams, following step 13 on page 17. Repeat with the lining.

9. Try on the patchwork jacket *with shoulder pads pinned in place* from the outside. Adjust the shoulder-pad placement as needed. Turn up and pin the desired sleeve hem allowance. Remove the jacket and press the hem allowance in place on the jacket sleeves. Stitch hems in place by hand.

10. Complete step 14 on page 17. Sew the shoulder pads to the shoulder seam by hand as shown in step 15 on page 17.

11. Trim $1/2$" from the bottom edge of the sleeve linings, then turn under and press $1/2$".

12. With right sides together, pin the jacket/collar unit to the lining/collar unit. Stitch $1/2$" from the raw edges, leaving an 8"-long opening at the center back on the bottom edge of the jacket for turning.

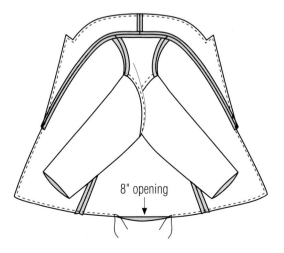

8" opening

Trim the seam to ¼", clip curves, and trim across collar points and lower front corners. Turn right side out, pushing the lining sleeves into the jacket sleeves. Press outer edges carefully, turning in the seam allowances at the back bottom opening. Slipstitch the opening closed.

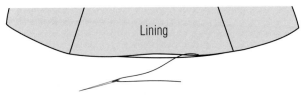

Slipstitch lining to piping.

13. Edgestitch or topstitch ¼" from the outer finished edges of the jacket and collar if desired. This will keep the lining from peeking to the outside of the jacket.

14. To hold the collar in position, hand sew the neckline seams of the jacket and the lining together in the well of the seam.

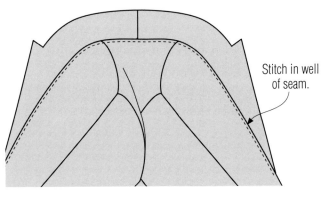

Stitch in well of seam.

15. On the right side of the finished collar, stitch soutache braid in place ¼" from the outer finished edge, carefully turning edges under to finish. See jacket on page 105.

16. Slipstitch the folded edge of the sleeve lining to the sleeve just below the upper edge of the sleeve hem allowance.

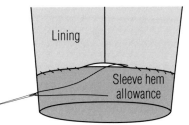

Lining

Sleeve hem allowance

17. Add buttons to the yoke fronts for embellishment as desired.

18. Add conchos, leather strips, and beads below the collar on each jacket front. Refer to the jacket in the photo on page 105.

Jacket Ten by Evelyn Dixon, Hallettsville, Texas. Metallic cording adds a little glitz to Evelyn's jacket.

Instead of making matching sleeves, Evelyn used Arrowhead leftovers for the right sleeve of her jacket. (See page 102.)

The Last Dance

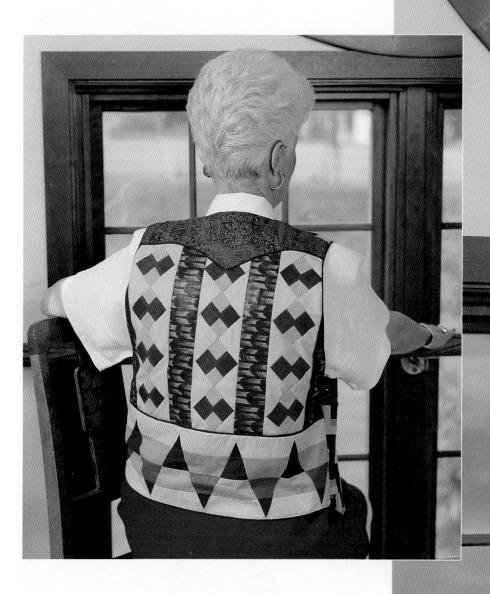

- ▬ **Four-Patch Reverse**

- ▬ **Rail Fence Frenzy**

- ▬ **Pieced Squares**

- ▬ **Seminole Strip**

- ▬ **Quick Random Patchwork**

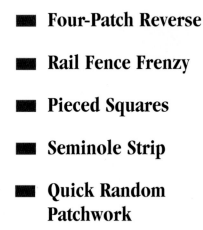

Here's a great way to use up all the leftovers from your jackets—a vest to complement any wardrobe. Your Last Dance Vest will be the finishing touch to denims for casual wear or to fancy fashion fabrics for party attire. Choose your favorite vest pattern or use the front and back pattern pieces for Jackets Six or Eight on the pullout pattern at the back of this book.

If you wish to wear your vest over blouses and T-shirts with deep armholes, you may stitch a deeper seam in the armhole from notch to notch under the arm. Do not do this until you have tested the fit over the garment you plan to wear with the vest. It's time to get out all your false starts and rejects and begin the last dance.

MATERIALS

Vest Foundation   1–1½ yds. cotton flannel or muslin
Vest Lining   1–1½ yds. silky fabric or smooth cotton
Interfacing   ¾ yd. lightweight fusible interfacing
Leftovers from your jackets, including patchwork pieces, threads, beads, fabrics, buttons, and trims

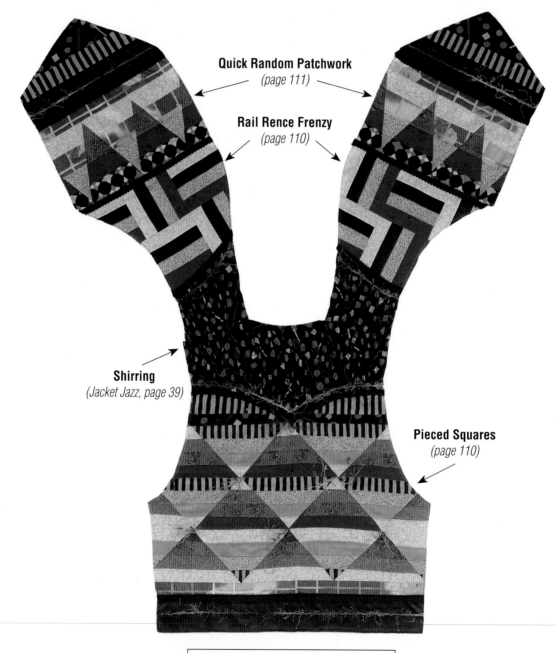

Quick Random Patchwork
(page 111)

Rail Rence Frenzy
(page 110)

Shirring
(Jacket Jazz, page 39)

Pieced Squares
(page 110)

Last Dance Vest by Judy Murrah

DIRECTIONS

1. Cut the vest fronts and back from the flannel or muslin foundation fabric. Use facing pattern pieces to cut interfacing pieces from fusible interfacing. Use leftovers or make a piece of patchwork using your favorite technique from one of the jackets. Position in a similar fashion as instructed for the jacket. For example, Jacket Six has a large Kaleidoscope piece left over. Make it the beginning of a vest. Place it on the back in the same way you did for the jacket and go on from there.

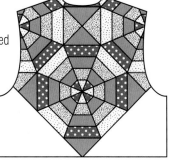

Patchwork leftovers positioned on vest back as they were in Jacket 6 (page 24)

OR

2. Go through the leftover pieces of techniques from any of the jackets you have made from this book and/or *Jacket Jazz*. Choose color combinations that appeal to you. Add strips and pieces of fabrics with these colors. I stack these pieces on a table and toss in and toss out as I go. It's fun to see what you can pull together from leftovers. For me, it's much more fun than trying to make something out of leftovers from my refrigerator.

3. If you wish, use the front and back yoke patterns from Jacket Ten. Draw these shapes onto the vest foundation. Cut the back and/or front yokes from any leftover patchwork piece that is large enough. Join 2 different patchwork designs to make the pieces large enough or cut the yoke shapes a little smaller. At any rate, this is another good place to start the process.

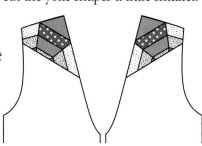

4. Work in sections or bands for the remainder of the vest. Piece segments together from false starts and rejects to make a new piece of patchwork or use some of the following techniques to make new fill-in patchwork pieces. Couch or topstitch decorative trims in place.

♪ **NOTE:** All of the following techniques require strips cut from the crosswise grain of the fabric.

Four-Patch Reverse

(See vest front on page 107.)

1. Sew 2 different strips of equal widths together along the long edges. Press the seam toward the darker of the 2 strips.

2. Cut the strip-pieced unit into sections the same width as the cut width of the individual strips. If you used $1^1/2$"-wide strips, cut the segments $1^1/2$" wide.

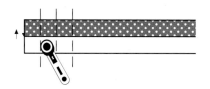

3. Sew 2 sections together as shown to create a Four-Patch block.

4. Sew the patches together in rows, then sew the rows together to make a piece of patchwork large enough to cover the desired area.

5. Pin to the foundation in the desired location and trim even with the raw edges. Stitch $^1/4$" from the raw edges. Refer to the photo of the vest on page 107.

Rail Fence Frenzy

1. Cut 1½"-wide strips from 4 different fabrics. (Strip length will vary, depending on the fabric leftovers you have available.)

2. Sew the 4 strips together along the long edges, using ¼"-wide seam allowances. Position the fabric strips with the most contrast in either the first or fourth position in the strip-pieced unit. The completed unit should be 4½" wide.

3. Crosscut the strip-pieced unit into 4½" squares.

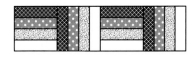

4. Sew the squares together into rows, reversing the strip direction in every other block. Refer to the photo of the vest on page 108.

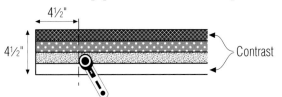

Pieced Squares

1. Cut a 1½"-wide strip from 4 different fabrics. From a fifth fabric, cut 2 strips, each 1½" wide. (Strip length will vary, depending on the fabric leftovers you have available.)

2. Sew the strips together in 2 units of 3 strips each, using a strip of the fifth fabric as the last strip in each. If you wish to cover a larger area with Pieced Squares, use 6 different fabrics plus a seventh fabric for the ends of each strip-pieced unit. Refer to the photo of the vest on page 108.

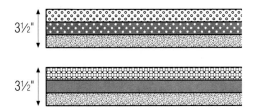

3. Cut triangles from the strip-pieced unit, using a 45° x 90° ruler. Triangles should be 6" long on the long side and 4" long on each of the 2 short sides.

Sew the triangles together into rows, alternating triangles cut from each strip-pieced unit. Sew 2 rows together so every other triangle forms a square.

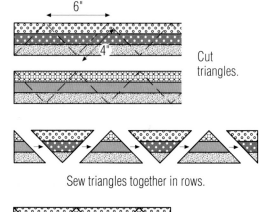

Cut triangles.

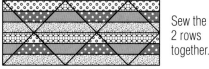

Sew triangles together in rows.

Sew the 2 rows together.

Seminole Strip

1. Select 4 different fabrics that coordinate with but also contrast with each other. Cut a 1½"-wide strip from each of 2 of the fabrics. From the third fabric, cut 2 strips, each ¾" wide. From the remaining fabric, cut 2 strips, each 2¾" wide.

2. Make a strip-pieced unit with 1 of the ¾"-wide strips between 2 of the 1½"-wide strips. Use ¼"-wide seams and press seams in one direction. Save the other strips for another step.

3. Crosscut the entire strip-pieced unit into 1½"-wide segments.

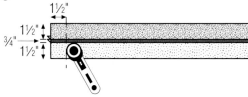

4. Cut the remaining ¾"-wide strip into 2¾" segments.

5. Join 2 of the units cut in step 3 above with a ¾" x 2¾" segment, reversing the direction of the second strip-pieced unit as shown.

Make as many of these units as possible from the pieces you have.

6. Cut the $2^3/_4$"-wide strips into $4^1/_2$" segments.

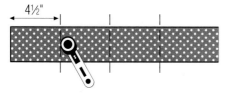

7. Sew a patchwork unit from step 5 between every $2^3/_4$" x $4^1/_2$" segment. Begin and end with a $4^1/_2$" rectangle.

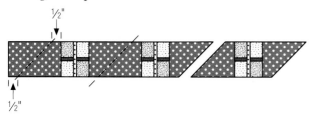

8. Cut the resulting strip into parallelograms, placing the ruler $1/_2$" from the seam line between each rectangle and patchwork unit as shown.

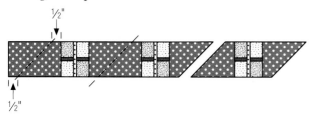

9. Sew the resulting pieces together, offsetting each strip so points of pieced squares line up. As you sew the segments together, determine how many segments you need in a row to cover the desired area on the vest front or back. You may use these pieces in vertical or horizontal rows. Trim each long edge, leaving a $1/_4$"-wide seam allowance beyond the points of the pieced squares.

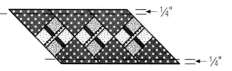

Quick Random Patchwork

1. Using strips of equal widths that you already have or that you cut from leftovers, make a strip-pieced unit. I used 4 strips, each 2" wide, per unit. The finished unit was $6^1/_2$" wide. Make a second unit, using different but coordinating fabrics.

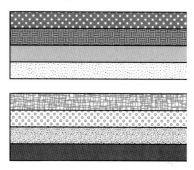

2. Cut the resulting strip-pieced units into triangles, using one of your special rulers—the Kaleidoscope, 9° Circle Wedge, or Clearview Triangle, for example.

3. Sew the pieces back together, alternating the strip combinations. Use to cover the desired area on the vest front or back. Refer to the photo of the vest on page 106.

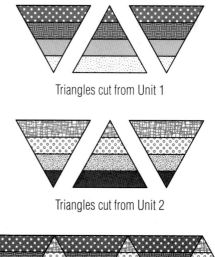

Triangles cut from Unit 1

Triangles cut from Unit 2

Sew pieces together, alternating units.

Vest Finishing

1. Fuse interfacing pieces to the wrong side of the vest fronts and back. Finish the raw edges of the patchwork pieces with your choice of gimp, braid, or piping as shown for the jacket in step 6 on page 16.

2. With right sides together, sew the vest fronts to the vest back at the shoulders, using a $1/2$"-wide seam allowance. Repeat with the lining. Press seams open. Add trim over shoulder seam line of vest if desired.

3. With right sides together, pin the lining to the vest, matching the shoulder seams and with all outer edges even. Stitch the lining to the vest, leaving the side seams open for turning. Clip the curves and corners.

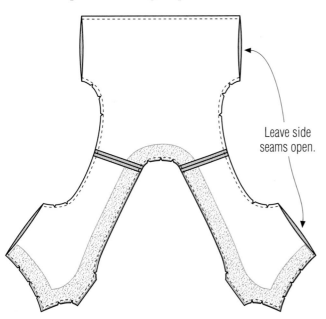

Leave side seams open.

4. Turn the vest right side out by pulling the fronts through the shoulders and out one of the back side openings as shown. Press carefully.

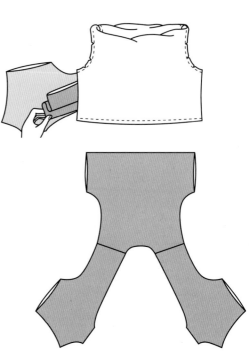

5. With right sides together and raw edges even, pin the vest front to the back at the sides, matching the armhole and lower edge seam lines. Starting on the lining 1" above the armhole seam, stitch the vest side seams, ending the stitching on the lining 1" below the seam at the bottom edge of the vest as shown.

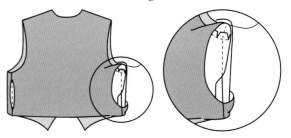

6. Press the side seams toward the vest back. Turn under the side seam allowances on the lining back and blindstitch to the lining along the front side seam allowance.

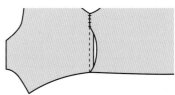

7. Press the vest one final time. Hang it on a hanger and give it the once-over to see if there's just one more doo-dad you could add. Then put that smart-looking thing on your back and take off like you're the hottest thing going. Have fun!

Vest by Judy Murrah, Victoria, Texas. This vest includes leftovers from Kaleidoscope Radiance, Strip-Stitched Scrappys, and Woven Patch closure. Judy embellished the vest with Prairie Points, trims, and antique buttons from her collection.

Vest by Barbara Terry, Houston, Texas. Barbara used Seminole Strips and Quick Random Patchwork on the front and back. She filled in the right front with leftover strips and pleating. The vest is embellished with decorative braids and trims, charms, beads, yo-yos, and a metallic gold tassel.

Judy Murrah learned to sew at an early age from her dear little 4-foot-11-inch-tall mother, and she's been exploring this fun and creative medium ever since. Judy learned to quilt in 1976 and soon she was teaching classes. Making new friends while sharing what she has learned is one of her most favorite things to do. She says, "I love to show my students how smart and talented they are. They are always so surprised with themselves."

At the very top of her list of favorite things to do is to get together with her young adult children and Tom, her husband of 28 years. Todd, her older son, is a Texas A&M graduate and restaurant manager in San Antonio. Holly, the only daughter in the trio, is at A&M majoring in Marketing and Management. Troy, the youngest, but also the tallest in the whole family, is an Architecture major at A&M.